Katharine Tynan

THE IRISH WRITERS SERIES
James F. Carens, General Editor

TITLE	*AUTHOR*
SEAN O'CASEY	Bernard Benstock
J. C. MANGAN	James Kilroy
W. R. RODGERS	Darcy O'Brien
STANDISH O'GRADY	Phillip L. Marcus
PAUL VINCENT CARROLL	Paul A. Doyle
SEUMAS O'KELLY	George Brandon Saul
SHERIDAN LEFANU	Michael Begnal
BRIAN FRIEL	D. E. S. Maxwell
DANIEL CORKERY	George Brandon Saul
EIMAR O'DUFFY	Robert Hogan
MERVYN WALL	Robert Hogan
FRANK O'CONNOR	James Matthews
JOHN BUTLER YEATS	Douglas Archibald
MARIA EDGEWORTH	James Newcomer
MARY LAVIN	Zack Bowen
SOMERVILLE AND ROSS	John Cronin
SUSAN L. MITCHELL	Richard M. Kain
J. M. SYNGE	Robin Skelton
KATHARINE TYNAN	Marilyn Gaddis Rose
LIAM O'FLAHERTY	James O'Brien
IRIS MURDOCH	Donna Gerstenberger
BENEDICT KIELY	Daniel J. Casey
DOUGLAS HYDE	Gareth Dunleavy
EDNA O'BRIEN	Grace Eckley
BRIAN MOORE	Jeanne Flood
ELIZABETH BOWEN	Edwin J. Kenney
JOHN MONTAGUE	Frank Kersnowski
CHARLES ROBERT MATURIN	Robert E. Lougy

KATHARINE TYNAN

Marilyn Gaddis Rose

Lewisburg

BUCKNELL UNIVERSITY PRESS

London: ASSOCIATED UNIVERSITY PRESSES

© 1974 by Associated University Presses, Inc.

Associated University Presses, Inc.
Cranbury, New Jersey 08512

Associated University Presses
108 New Bond Street
London W1Y OQX, England

Library of Congress Cataloging in Publication Data
Rose, Marilyn Gaddis.
  Katharine Tynan.

  (The Irish writers series)
  Bibliography: p.
  1.   Hinkson, Katharine (Tynan) 1861–1931.
PR4790.H3Z83   1974   821'.9'12   71–126276
ISBN 0–8387–7770–8
ISBN 0–8387–7771–6 (pbk.)

Contents

Acknowledgments

The author makes grateful acknowledgment to Miss Pamela Hinkson for permission to use copyrighted material by Katharine Tynan; Miss Hinkson was most gracious also in answering questions about her mother. The author is grateful to Mr. Michael B. Yeats for permission to quote from W. B. Yeats, *Letters to Katharine Tynan,* edited by Roger McHugh; to Mr. Yeats and The Macmillan Company of New York for permission to quote from the *Autobiography of William Butler Yeats*; to Macmillan & Company, Ltd., London, for permission to quote from Joseph Hone, *W. B. Yeats.* The portrait of Katharine Tynan by John Butler Yeats is reproduced by courtesy of the Municipal Gallery of Modern Art, Dublin; the National Gallery of Ireland; and Miss Ann Butler Yeats and Mr. Michael B. Yeats, heirs of John Butler Yeats.

Chronology

1861   Katharine is born, January 23, one of Andrew Cullen and Elizabeth Reilly Tynan's eleven children to live past infancy, County Dublin.

1868,   approximately. Her family moves to Whitehall, Clondalkin, her home until marriage.

1875,   approximately. Her formal education completed at fourteen, she leaves the Dominican Convent of St. Catherine of Siena, Drogheda.

1878   She publishes her first poem and joins the Land League under the guidance of Anna Parnell.

1885   She publishes her first of more than eighty titles, a book of poems, *Louise de la Vallière and Other Poems*. She meets W. B. Yeats.

1887,   approximately. She begins writing prose.

1891   Political fall and subsequent death of Parnell.

1893   Marriage to Henry Albert Hinkson and beginning of eighteen-year sojourn in England. After the deaths of their first two children in infancy, they have two sons and a daughter: Theobald Henry (d. 1968), Giles Aylmer ("Pat") (d. 1957), Pamela Mary.

1911   Return to Ireland when Mr. Hinkson is named
        Resident Magistrate for County Mayo.
1914   She "attends" World Congress of Women in
        Rome in the Spring.
1916   Easter Week.
1919   Death of Mr. Hinkson, January 11.
1919–23 Extensive travel in British Isles and Western
        Europe, including three long stays in Cologne.
1931   Death in London, April 2, after brief illness.

Introduction

During Katharine Tynan's lifetime (1861–1931), her listing in *Who's Who* stated that her recreations were "talking to a good listener, companionship of dogs, society of children." These three sources of satisfaction, which show her lighthearted spoofing of a pompous questionnaire, tell us more about her than she probably realized! She was a person for whom life was a process that depended upon the *other*. Although writing is a solitary act, for her it was not the product of solitary study of the self. Her "good listener" was often the writer's imaginary listener, and for her, he and particularly *she* comprised a reading audience. As a girl, she wrote to please her father, to encourage her friends, to let her own serene soul commune sympathetically with characters in history and legend. As a wife and mother, Mrs. Henry Albert Hinkson, she wrote for her family, and when I say that she wrote for a living, I mean "living" in the fullest sense: the household needed her livelihood, but writing had become by then an integral part of living for her. As a widowed career woman, she wrote for her public and, since its members were so close to her in station and tastes, she wrote as an outlet for her own fears, fantasies,

opinions, and causes also. She wrote, then, to express
what was generally applicable in her experiences as a
daughter, married woman, and mother.

Katharine Tynan, in short, is a woman writer who
sees herself and expresses herself in terms of women's
roles. As to what a woman's role is or has to be, she
begrudgingly accommodates herself to the functional
definitions established by male consensus. In her
poetry, her most rigorously controlled genre by any set
of standards, her low expectations of every man
outside her own family are not completely sublimated,
but they are so conventionally disguised that they would
neither offend a male reader nor alarm a female reader.
In her fiction, her least controlled genre, her plots
and characterizations are woven with implicit criticism
of men's inevitable inadequacies, with which women's
resourcefulness must forever cope. In her journalism,
she is quite explicit that a man's world is not the best
of all possible worlds for a woman.

During the fifty-three years of her career, women
succeeded in getting men to redefine women's roles,
legally at any rate. In her poetry there is no reflection
of the marked changes in the feminine climate. Her
poems perhaps become more asexual once her own
children are reared, so that in the end she is, once
again as in girlhood, gently eulogizing, "nostalgizing"
her internalized ideal of Ireland, quietly predicating
the stability of her Roman Catholic faith. Her postwar
fiction reveals implicitly, perhaps even inadvertently,
her mixed feelings about the new freedoms. Her father had
provided her a secure suburban salon in the late 1880s. But
in the 1920s, she, a working widow with seriously

defective eyesight, accompanied her attractive, intrepid daughter Pamela around western Europe on their journalistic assignments at a time when a sojourn home meant keeping alive while a civil war raged. She knew that pluck and prudence often had to be supplemented by Providence, when the new woman went out on her own, and her novels explore catastrophes, like abduction and sequestration, that she and Pamela managed to avoid. Her journalistic writing, and this includes her memoirs, which are connected feature stories about other people rather than any attempt at self-analysis, shows how she succeeded in a man's world and how she proposed to make it easier for other women to succeed also.

Thus, she writes to women, about women, and on behalf of women, and when she writes directly about herself, it is only as a slightly exceptional, somewhat encouraging example of a type.

She eschews self-analysis altogether. On the one hand, this is commendable, for it means that she does not indulge in self-pity or waste time with personal problems that cannot be solved. On the other hand, she may have hampered the development of her own genius, for at times in her memoirs she seems to lack self-awareness. As a writer, she does not seem to have been capable of self-criticism. In her work there are frequent slips that show an uncritical acceptance of class prejudices. When she avoids plumbing her own depths, she may well prevent herself from knowing anyone else in depth.

In the final analysis, having a complete gamut of experiences available to women of her class helped

Katharine Tynan to find a market, but it seems to have been no advantage in the development of her gifts. Just the mention of certain other women writers of her generation—Emilia Pardo Bazan, Selma Lagerlöff, Clara Viebig, Edith Wharton, Richarda Huch—shows how limited her vision was. Countess Pardo Bazan, despite the restrictions of a Spanish noblewoman's life, promoted Zolaesque Naturalism in a convincing delineation of the decline of the Spanish gentry. Miss Lagerlöff, a Nobel Prize winner, incorporated into her novels the polarities of folkloric fantasizing and grim egoistic hardheadedness found (or so we deduce from her novels) in Swedish character. Miss Viebig, referred to as the German Zola, depicted the misery of the disadvantaged classes. Mrs. Wharton, aside from the *tour de force* of *Ethan Frome,* relentlessly, albeit sympathetically, studied the refined maladjustments of her own class, the Manhattan *haute bourgeoisie.* Miss Huch, responsive to the changing tempers of styles and subjects, a onetime Expressionist, could express the plight of the self and the collective self in her lyric poetry and prose epics. I have summarized the contributions of these good writers, who happen to have been women, in terms that will keep in mind Katharine Tynan's opportunities in style and subject. The Ireland and England of her lifetime furnished her analogous materials that were just as rich and possibly more distinctive. Certainly there was more basic drama in Clondalkin than in Manhattan; the problem of sheer survival surely takes precedence over the complexes caused by affluence. The rise of nationalism, the revival that was virtually a rescue from extinction of

Celtic language and civilization, and the persistance of Ascendancy traditions additionally were available to her. But her pen did not fix them for posterity.

It may seem unfair to compare her with her international contemporaries, other women formed by the nineteenth century but living well into the twentieth. They have an international reputation to which she never aspired. I should instead mention Irish women of her generation, writers who have had, like her, a much more limited audience. These would include Lady Gregory, Susan Mitchell, Dora Sigerson, Eleanor Hull, E. O. Somerville, and Martin Ross. Here the simple juxtaposition of her name and theirs does not eclipse hers. Katharine Tynan's best poems will easily stand comparison with those of Susan Mitchell, Dora Sigerson, and Eleanor Hull. She excels them in facility and range. However, it could not be demonstrated that in her prose she ever equals Lady Gregory or Somerville and Ross. These three women express a more authentic picture both of their Anglo-Irish class and of the surrounding "mere" Irish. When dealing with the humbler Irish classes, they can report only the exterior, but they set up a framework that permits an outside view. To return again to Mrs. Hinkson's *Who's Who* recreations, these three women seem to have been good listeners.

Better than she? Not necessarily. It all depends upon the speaker. Somerville and Ross and Lady Gregory had a better ear for common folk speech and, being members of the upper stratum of the Ascendancy, they could reproduce their own speech. But Mrs. Hinkson, Roman Catholic, rural-suburban, upper middle class, could speak in her own voice and find a ready listener. And she could speak as the loving daughter, dutiful wife, and fond mother.

To appraise Katharine Tynan as a writer would not be worthwhile if we examined solely literary merit. Yeats is the only member of the first generation of the group associated with *Poems and Ballads of Young Ireland* (1888) whose work has survived. Nor would it be worthwhile to appraise her solely for her membership in this generation. She was not associated with it long enough. And certainly the reigning woman of the Irish Renaissance was Lady Gregory. Nor can we see her as the center of a circle, as has been done with her older friend, Alice Meynell. She had the semblance of a salon when she lived with her father, but after she was married, she lacked the means for entertaining. It becomes clear from her own account that, many as her friends were—and everyone attests to her capacity for warm friendship—and skilled as she was as a hostess, she had to be a guest. She had to be the literary lioness in other hostesses' salons. She was most welcome; her charm, tact, and gift of anecdote made her an excellent talker for the good listener. In my view, it will be fairest and the most informative if I appraise her work as a woman writer, as an exemplar of her class and sex at her moment in time.

Her popularity is a gauge of English and Irish taste, especially female and middle class, during the first three decades of this century. She was one with her readers. It was second nature for her to voice their ideals in her poetry and to flatter their aspirations and rationalize their prejudices in her prose. She described her readers' virtues knowingly and exposed their limitations, I suspect, inadvertently. Katharine Tynan was at home in the atmosphere that Yeats found exasperating, that Joyce found unendurable.

Let us look at Katharine Tynan's work in terms of her consecutive roles—first, as her father's girl and as the hostess who encouraged the young men of the Irish Renaissance with her precocious publishing and ready hospitality; second, as the wife and mother who wrote, as her daughter remembers, for "hearth and home"; finally, as the determined widow whose writing had to be her life. As her role changed, so did her expression of it; as the lives of middle-class women changed, so did their expectations as readers. She met the challenge with ease. Since I am treating her as an illustration of middle-class taste and commitments, I shall be obliged to take up not only her most carefully written poems but some of her most carelessly written novels also. Her works will illuminate a set of values in which the recreations are those afforded by visiting friends, comforting animals, and mothering children.

1

1861–1893: The Daughter

"Everything that I made I used to bring to you."

Kate and her father, Andrew C. Tynan, gentleman farmer and farming entrepreneur, lived for and through each other. Their affectionate mutual dependency was, of course, unmarred by Freudian second thoughts. But a reader is struck by the exclusiveness of the devotion in this relationship. From her creative works and from the bulk of Kate's autobiographical writings, we could easily deduce that she was the only child of a long-widowed father. The novel *The Playground* (1930) has a secondary plot that carries the conviction of autobiography and is the story of a girl whose relatively late marriage left her farmer father very lonely. However, she was not a widower's only child. She mentions early in the first volume of her memoirs, *Twenty-five Years* (London, 1913), that "baby succeeded baby rapidly in the home of my childhood till we were eleven living" (p. 23). She states a few pages further, "My mother was a large, placid, fair woman, who became an invalid at an early age and influenced my life scarcely at all" (p. 27). Thereafter, she drops her mother as a subject, mentioning that she owned a great deal of pretty china and that she tried to keep her weak-eyed daughter from reading novels.

Kate's siblings are even more shadowy. She occasionally admits that there was a sister about. But no sibling other than an older sister Mary, who died in the autumn of 1868 before she could begin her novitiate, is ever identified by name or mentioned with either precision or tenderness. In *The Middle Years* (London, 1916), Mrs. Tynan Hinkson devotes a chapter to the congenial Cork barrister John O'Mahony, who, she says, "married a younger sister of mine" in 1895 (p. 163). We receive a strong impression that in her spiritual world she simply "factored out" every family member other than her father. In her poem "Everything that I Made" she assures him that he is the center of her world: "Was it a song, why, then, 'twas a song to sing to you./ Was it a story, to you I was telling my story" [*The Poems of Katherine [sic] Tynan*, ed. Monk Gibbon, Dublin, 1963].

It was perhaps easier for Kate to isolate herself in her own world because of her severe visual handicap. During some two-year period of the late 1860's, she was stricken by a chronic ulcerated-eye condition, probably the aftermath of measles. Her agonized father took her to a round of specialists until the ulcers were cured. However, she never knew normal vision again. She was, we deduce from her testimony, extremely myopic. She continually refers to herself as "purblind." This limited range of vision encouraged her natural bent to preoccupation and meditation, so that another person was often almost upon her before she was aware of him. We know from her gift for description that she was extremely responsive to color, and her poem "The Purblind Praises the Lord" expresses her appreciation of mass

("Pink blossom on the apple-branch/For me's a rosy bower") and deprecation of detail ("I miss the common and the dull,/The small details of things"). We know also that once a person came into her range of vision, she was acutely impressionable and very accurate in rendering her impressions. We can validate her eyewitness testimony easily by citing her remarks in *Twenty-five Years* about two famous friends of hers during this stage of her career. The elegant British poetess Alice Meynell struck her "as a beautiful pale face, ivory as the crescent moon and lit by the most wonderful eyes, in masses of dark hair" (p. 126). Willie Yeats at twenty was "tall and lanky," "beautiful to look at with his dark face, its touch of vivid colouring, the night-black hair, the eager dark eyes" (pp. 143–44). Her handicapped vision did not interfere with her reading and certainly did not discourage it. She read voraciously and lived vicariously in the private world that her father protected.

When their bustling, comfortable home, Whitehall in Clondalkin, did not seem conducive to her development, he sent her to the Dominican Convent of St. Catherine of Siena at Drogheda. She left there when she was fourteen, her formal education, if it can be called that, completed. She adored the unworldly convent atmosphere and, for over a decade following her sister Mary's death in 1868, considered being a nun, but she had no illusions about the quality of the education that she received.

The convent did provide her an outlet for her natural capacity for affection. She discusses her first infatuation with disarming candor in *Twenty-five Years:*

> We had our little passions.... Mine was a passion
> for an elder girl about to become a nun.... I used to
> cry a great deal at night because she was going away,
> and she used to come and comfort me. I knew her
> footstep in the corridor and I used to feel faint with
> love when she came.... In the dark corridor on the
> way to Mass, as we passed the warm kitchen, ... she
> came behind me and kissed me. Oh, rapture! Oh,
> delight, Oh ecstasy! Was there anything in more
> mature passions quite as good? (p. 157)

She got over this infatuation, of course, and was to
have many affectionate friendships with women
throughout her life.

When she returned home from the convent, she
became her father's official companion and accompanied
him to plays, political meetings, and other events. She
published her first poem in 1878. She joined the Ladies
Land League and came under the beneficently broadening
influence of Miss Anna Parnell, sister of her hero and
idol. She collected her published poems and with the
efficient intercession of Wilfred Meynell published
Louise de la Vallière and Other Poems in 1885. Her
father had unhesitatingly paid Kegan, Paul, and Trench
twenty pounds to subsidize publication, but her volume
sold well, went quickly into a second edition, and she was
launched, to be a well-received author the rest of her life.

Her father had no rivals that either he or she recognized,
because her warmest relations during these years were
with other women. She was very fond of the poetesses
Dora Sigerson and Frances Wynne, but the editor Rosa
Mulholland "re-awoke the idealising passion which in
my schooldays I had given to my first love. I have had
few things in my life more exquisite than those afternoons

I used to spend with her" (she had been married nineteen years when she wrote this). Of the moments spent with both Miss Mulholland and the historian Sarah Atkinson she says, ". . .the door opened: we passed into an atmosphere which had something heavenly about it" (pp. 105–6).

As a girl launched on her career, sponsored by Father Mathew Russell, editor of the *Irish Monthly*, as an intimate of the Meynells, a visitor of Christina Rossetti and Lady Wilde, it was inevitable that she meet W. B. Yeats. She remembered Willie as a gentle creature who "lived, breathed, ate, drank and slept poetry" and confesses that "we all bullied Willie Yeats" (p. 145). Since it is known that he spent a great deal of time at Whitehall, that they saw each other frequently at other people's houses, especially that of John and Ellen O'Leary, and that he escorted her to literary and political evenings, there has been some speculation about a romance. It seems very unlikely. Joseph Hone, in his book on Yeats (New York, 1949, p. 62), states that Yeats wondered whether it was his duty to propose to her, and Roger McHugh on the basis of the unpublished autobiographical materials of Yeats believes that the young man thought she was in love with him (see *Letters to Katharine Tynan* [New York, 1953] p. 13). But he was not in love with her, and she, with her heart full of her father and female friends, could not have encouraged him.

Hone describes her rather unchivalrously as a "red-haired, homely, short-sighted girl of eager admiring disposition" (p. 58), but in John B. Yeats's portrait of her, painted in 1886 and later relinquished to the Dublin Municipal Gallery at the insistence of Hugh Lane, she looks sturdily good-looking. Her russet hair is arranged in becoming bangs on her forehead, her nose is strong and straight, her sensuous lips are parted almost provocatively, and her pince-nez only accentuates a steady gaze. Of course, the elder Yeats liked her and her spritely conversation, so he would have given her her best face, as only a friend could know it, and during the course of a typically extended Yeats sitting she became very friendly with the family, especially the girls, Lily and Lolly.

W. B. Yeats, who even at the time of his most esoteric enthusiasms still had a tough-minded streak, was bound to see that this girl four years older could offer him something. She embodied stability, comfort, modest affluence. But the two could hardly have agreed unanimously on anything except the superiority of Charles Stewart Parnell. An ardent Catholic, she could no more have accepted his nominal Protestantism than his investigations of the esoteric, which horrified when they did not amuse her. His impetuosity, his preoccupation required a wife who would be a caretaker, not a competitor. In the late 1880s, when their ages made a marriage appropriate, he was not, in the fullest sense of the cliché, good enough for her: he had no prospects.

They had known each other approximately four years before he wrote, October 10, 1889: "My dear Miss Tynan (I wonder if it would matter if I put your Christian name, by the bye?)" (*Letters,* p. 101). He wrote another letter before he received the one that apparently gave him permission to say "My dear Katey," November 6, 1889, for he wrote to her far more often than she wrote to him. He signed himself variously "Your friend,"

"Yours always," "Your friend always," but never other than "W. B. Yeats." Our only indication that she felt the slightest bit of possessiveness about him, perhaps a somewhat romantic motherliness, is the defense of his acquaintance with Maud Gonne, March 21, 1889. He met the fatal woman of his life, we note, a considerable time before he asked for permission to call Miss Tynan "Katey," and this suggests that he asked for a sign of intimacy at a time when he no longer had any real interest in presuming upon it. He defends himself thus: "Who told you that I am 'taken up with Miss Gonne'? I think she is very good-looking and that is all I think about her. . . . I sympathise with her love of the national idea . . . but care not much for the kind of Red Indian feathers in which she has trapped out that idea." He plays down the intensity of the impression Maud Gonne made on him by continuing, " . . . she had a borrowed interest, reminded me of Laura Armstrong without Laura's wild dash of half-insane genius. . ." (Laura was his cousin, with whom he had been infatuated). And now that he has erased one cause for Katey's apprehension or jealousy by reminding her of an earlier cause for apprehension, he can proceed to reassure her, "Will you forgive me having talked of her [Laura]? She interests me far more than Miss Gonne does and yet only as a myth and a symbol" (pp. 89–90). With Miss Gonne presumably buried in Katey's psyche under the dead love affair with Laura, he can get on to more important things, namely her help in getting him good reviews of his work.

For of one thing there is no doubt: their friendship was mutually useful for their literary ambitions. To him,

her considerable contacts with periodicals and newspapers were to prove more helpful than her free meals,
small loans, and genial banter. He was from the first her
most astute critic and was to prove a stellar *objet* in her
collection of famous friends.

Literary historians link their work in the Young Ireland
circle, the nomenclature taken from *Poems and Ballads
of Young Ireland,* 1888, which vies with Yeats's *The
Wandering of Oisin,* 1889, as the publishing event
inaugurating the Irish Renaissance. These poets included
Douglas Hyde; T. W. Rolleston, editor of *The Dublin
University Review;* John Todhunter; a poetess, Rose
Kavanagh, who was one of Kate's friends; and Kate
and Willie. Many like Kate had been favored by Father
Russell, who as remarked above, edited *The Irish Monthly.*
Hyde's reputation as a pioneer in modern Gaelic literature is important, and, obviously, as a patriot and
politician, he is quite secure. But we remember all of
them as writers chiefly because in the beginning they
were clustered around Yeats.

Kate, for one, was grateful for his influence, although,
it must be confessed, we can see little effect of his good
advice. In *Twenty-five Years* she pays this tribute: " . . . he
was 'the onlie begetter' of the new Irish poetry. Heaven
knows what rubbish he delivered us from! We were
all writing like the poets of a country newspaper,
copying a simplicity of the older poets which had long
ceased to be simple, aiming at a rhetorical passion which
had never been sincere. . . Willie Yeats did the spadework.
He cleared the ground" (p. 255).

Yeats was very tactful in his criticism, but he managed
to point out her failings all the same. Consider what he

wrote, December 21, 1888, about her Kinsale ballad:
"I . . . do not think it one of your very best. . . . I am
not very fond of retrospective art. . . . Your 'St. Francis'
was not retrospective, the St. Francis within you spoke."
He presents her inability to empathize, " . . . you have
tried to express feelings quite different from those
habitual with you, and have as a result described
things from without—more picturesquely than poetical-
ly." He softens his criticism with a compliment as he
continues, "Your old knight, however, I think is very
fine—but as to the rest, you have sacrificed all things
to colour. In the last ballad before this, 'The Children
of Lir,' the colour is most rich but it is not put in for its
own sake." "Your best work," he says as he inserts
a vital qualification, "—and no woman poet of the time
has done better—is always where you express your own
affectionate nature or your religious feeling, either
directly or indirectly in some legend." We are forced
to remember that no poetess of Kate's generation was
very good, and that Yeats knew it. He adds, now that
he has paid his compliment, "your worst, that . . . where
you allow your sense of colour to run away with you and
make you merely a poet of the picturesque." He makes
his final criticism palatable by sharing it: "The want
of your poetry is, I think, the want also of my own. We
both of us need to substitute more and more the landscapes of nature for the landscapes of art. . . . It is
curious—do forgive me all this—that your other fault,
that of sometimes a little overstating the emotion, is
only present when your landscapes are those of art"
(pp. 75–76).

Nearly a quarter century later, June 19, 1913, he

repeats that she should write about what she knows: "I think you are at your best when you write as a mother and when you remember your old home and the Dublin mountains." Only a decade away from the Nobel Prize, he let her share in his success as he specified that "we— you and I chiefly—have made a change [in taste] and brought into fashion in Ireland a less artless music" (p. 148).

Her later poetry supported the validity of his criticism, although the marks of his influence are not especially discernible. That is, when she was to write about the quiet pleasures of motherhood, simple strains of nostalgia for Ireland of the past, the uncomplicated devotional impulses of a simple, unquestioning Catholicism, then she was at her best. When she broached larger issues, she could not find the proper voice. Her poetic facility makes her lack of intellect all the more apparent. But, as we shall see later, *The Holy War*, which by current standards is an embarrassing book, was to be one of her most popular and influential volumes. For her own economic needs she took his advice only as she should.

Literary history has sided with him. By 1916, when Ernest Boyd published the first major overview of Anglo-Irish literature in *Ireland's Literary Renaissance*, her place as a poetess was already settled. Boyd commends her use of Irish materials, singles her out as the "only important Catholic poet in Ireland," but judges her a minor poet (see rev. ed., 1922, pp. 103–12).

Of her fiction no Yeats critique survives, but we can easily imagine the corollary of his passing comment in his letter of February 27, 1890, " . . . your prose style is

often so very good . . . Lady Wilde praised your prose
style again to me yesterday" (p. 111). Whatever Yeats may
have thought of her fiction, she had already discovered
that she had a profitable bent for it. She credits Alfred
Williams of the *Providence Journal* (Rhode Island) with setting her to writing prose in 1887. She had a flair for
chatty, semi-gossipy reporting and wholesome fiction.

Although she and Yeats were never estranged, their
lives and interests drew them apart, especially after her
marriage in 1893. On November 11, 1913, after Kate
had printed extensive extracts from his letters in *Twenty-
five Years*, he asked Lady Gregory to get the book from
the library: "It contains—without permission—pages
of my letters written when I was twenty-one or two . . .
The book, which is careless and sometimes stupid,
contains a great deal that moves me, for it is a very
vivid picture of the Dublin of my youth" (Hone, *W. B.
Yeats*, pp. 291–92). Kate, whom he now calls Mrs.
Hinkson, must have had some qualms, for he reassures
her a month later, "No, you were not very indiscreet,
though you were a little" (*Letters*, p. 149). She worked
many another of his letters into *The Middle Years* (1916),
although they were mostly written before 1891, when
the second volume of her memoirs begins. In 1920,
apparently judging that she had no further use for the
letters, she sold them to an American dealer for one
hundred pounds, and thereby, I am tempted to add, put
a terminal date on their friendship.

Yeats waited fifteen years to close his books on their
friendship, when he edited the *Oxford Book of Modern
Verse* in 1936. He gave ample space to Anglo-Irish and
Scotch poets and gallantly gave women their due. He

was open to the charge of looking out for his particular friends when he included poems by Lady Gregory, Dorothy Wellesley, and Margot Ruddock. He did not include a single poem by "Katey" Tynan. (Other women in the volume are Katharine Bradley, Mary Elizabeth Coleridge, Edith Cooper, Frances Cornford, Alice Meynell, and Vivian de Sola Pinto.)

Katharine Tynan's role in the Irish Renaissance, then, seems to reduce itself to this: a briefly associated minor talent. For a while she was a close friend of its genius. Although it appeared, in the early days, that she might at least aspire to being its best "woman writer," by the turn of the century Lady Gregory had taken that position and would keep it. At the same time that she was growing further away from the Irish in-group of the generation of the nineties, she was growing closer to writers with whom she had more in common: Francis Thompson, whom she met through his benefactors and her good friends Wilfred and Alice Meynell, and Dora Sigerson Shorter, to mention only those who have kept a place in literary history. These people were devout like her and had no place in their belief for the mysticism of Yeats or AE. In the long run she would feel more at home with writers who looked on life as a part of God's Plan.

Louise de la Vallière and Other Poems (1885) shows clearly not only her simple orthodox Catholic orientation but also her feminine outlook. Early reviewers discerned Pre-Raphaelite characteristics, although her own reading of those poets had been slight and unsystematic during the period of composition. It would be more accurate to say that she shared the fashionable interests and tastes

of the mid-1880s. The volume contains four monologues
—in the Browning manner—of heroines in history and
legend: Louise de la Vallière, Joan of Arc, King
Cophetua's Queen, Vivia Perpetua. There is a monologue,
"Waiting," done in the manner of Longfellow, whom
Katharine Tynan admired very much; it is spoken by a
prehistoric giant who awaits the hour of Ireland's
redemption, when he will emerge from his Donegal
cavern and do battle under Finn. King Cophetua's
beggar queen, an appealing subject for an unmarried
girl, was immortalized by Sir Edward Burne-Jones's
famous painting, 1884, the year Kate's book went to
press. Her poem "A Tired Heart" suggests that her
visualization of Christ had been influenced by Hugh
Holman Hunt's "Light of the World" (1851–54), for
Christ, who is the speaker of the poem, has Anglo-
Saxon coloring: "On My gold head the dews have left
a stain."

All her poems in this collection give evidence of an
impressive facility with language. They would conform
admirably to lay preconceptions of poetry. The diction
is chaste, in tone that of English poetry since William
Collins. It rarely exceeds the rhyming license allowed
to popular ballad. Yet the diction is not that of any level
of speech, colloquial or formal. This is somewhat
surprising when the poems are either monologues of an
adopted *persona* or of herself as a *persona*. No one, not
even she herself, speaks in character. Her poetic voice
speaks the way a "poet" is supposed to. For example, in
"Thoreau at Walden" she exclaims from her impressions,
which are either based on misinformation or wrenched by
a misguided concession to rhyme:

Seeking this sage in fair fraternity
Came Hawthorne here and Emerson, I know.
O happy woods, that watched them to and fro!

The conjunction of "happy woods" and "to and fro" makes it seem as if these three men frolicked like adolescents in the woods, unless it was the woods' watching that was "to and fro." The only two words that really fit here are "sage" and "fraternity." We are justified in quibbling about virtually every other expression, for example, in what sense was the fraternity "fair"? why invert the verbs "Came Hawthorne here"? What has happened is that the loose iambic rhythm of prose has been sacrificed for a strained, strict iambic to make the line "poetic" in the most pedestrian sense of the word. I have not been concentrating on these random lines to show that Kate was a bad poet but to show what the uncritical public liked and bought, what, say, her father and girl friends would think sounded good. She claims in *The Middle Years* that her publisher Kegan Paul "used to say that mine was the only poetry that sold with him. My name had been fragrant in the presbyteries and community-rooms" (pp. 100–101).

The public liked poems on subjects of decorous sentimentality, preferably of a religious cast, and the public wanted the poems to sound poetic, that is, have a regular beat and obvious rhymes. I must add in fairness to her and to her readers that if these two conditions of decorum and sound were met, they liked a good poem just as well. *Shamrocks* (1887) had more, better poems, including "St. Francis to the Birds," one of her most appealing poems. Indeed, there was to be a steady improvement in her poems up through *Innocencies* in 1905. To see her earliest poetry at its best, let us look at "The Children of Lir," the poem Yeats referred to when he wanted to show her how she wrote when she was at her best. This poem, which capitalizes on the legend of the princes and princesses turned into swans by their stepmother eons ago, is additionally a representative product of the Irish generation of the nineties. It uses Pre-Raphaelite techniques to tell a sad tale and arouse a melancholy mood.

While this ballad praises the values of living, it celebrates also the mystique of oppression. The episode of the Children of Lir, which could easily be seen as an allegory of Ireland since the advent of the Normans, shows the cosmic compensation for misfortune: special existence for the star-crossed heroes, special vision for their humble witnesses. And it is the special property of Irish twilight that vouchsafes the telling of this tale. When Irish penumbra blurs the sharp boundary lines between night and day, then the privileged story-teller can see emerge the contours of the fairy mid-world.

As such a privileged narrator, Kate begins by establishing a setting in which the supernatural is probable:

> Out upon the sand-dune thrive the coarse long grasses,
> Herons standing knee-deep in the brackish pool,
> Overhead the sunset fire and flame amasses,
>   And the moon to eastward rises pale and cool:
> Rose and green around her, silver-grey and pearly,
>   Chequered with the black rooks flying home to bed;
> For, to wake at daybreak, birds must couch them early,
>   And the day's a long one since the dawn was red.

Here Kate's language and meter fit her subject. It is
both dignified and artificial, yet not inaccurate for the
Irish landscape at twilight. In line 3 the grammatical
order implied is probably "the sunset amasses fire and
flame overhead," although the caesural pause after
"sunset" leads us first to suppose that "fire and flame"
is a compound noun using a singular, intransitive verb
"amasses." A comma after "overhead" might prevent
a reader from giving grammatical significance to the
caesural pause. The last two lines serve chiefly to
complete the double quatrain. The first quatrain is
narrated impersonally; from "home to bed" to the end
of the stanza we have homely details that show a
domestic perspective. It is as if a mother were telling
her child, reluctant to go to bed, that the birds are
tired out after a long day. "Couch them," which sounds
like a Gallicism today, was rare in the late nineteenth
century, and "are nesting" would be more accurate and
more idiomatic. However, such words prepare us for the
sympathy that we are expected to have for the Children
of Lir, whom the narrator, moving her camera eye
from panorama to focused subject, picks up in the
second stanza:

> On the chilly lakelet, in that pleasant gloaming,
>   See the sad swans sailing: they shall have no rest:
> Never a voice to greet them save the bittern's booming
>   Where the ghostly sallows sway against the West.

The scene is pleasing to the eye ("pleasant gloaming"),
but the swans are sad, and we know they are the
Children of Lir when the narrator repeats the decree
"they shall have no rest." We are now close enough to

pick up the dialogue, which completes the identification:

"Sister," saith the grey swan, "Sister, I am weary,"
　Turning to the white swan wet, despairing eyes;
"O," she saith, "my young one. O," she saith, "my dearie,"
　Casts her wings about him with a storm of cries.

We presume that Kate used "saith" because she considered it softer sounding than "said." That is her prerogative. Most of the time, however, she uses the modern third person. Then the narrator gives us a résumé of the legend in the third stanza:

Woe for Lir's sweet children, whom their vile stepmother
　Glamoured with her witch-spells for a thousand years;
Died their father raving, on his throne another,
　Blind before the end came from the burning tears.
Long the swans have wandered over lake and river.
　Gone is all the glory of the race of Lir,
Gone and long forgotten like a dream of fever;
　But the swans remember the sweet days that were.

The second line, which reads very smoothly, has a curious juxtaposition in levels of language. "Glamour," even when used incorrectly as a verb as here, is sophisticated; "witch-spells" is a folksy compound. "Enchanted with her witchery," for example, while probably no better, would have kept a unified tone. Line 4 would be a lot clearer for novices in Celtic lore if she had specified whose "burning tears." "Dream of fever" is undoubtedly not "dream about fever" but "dream during fever," an image that fourscore years of medical progress have made almost unintelligible to a modern reader, and "dream in fever" might be grammatically clearer.

The narrator then introduces and individualizes each Child of Lir:

Hugh, the black and white swan with the beauteous feathers,
　Fiachra, the black swan with the emerald breast,
Conn, the youngest, dearest, sheltered in all weathers,
　Him his snow-white sister loves the tenderest.
These her mother gave her as she lay a-dying
　To her faithful keeping; faithful hath she been,
With her wings spread o'er them when the tempest's crying,
　And her songs so hopeful when the sky's serene.

(Using "the tenderest" adverbially instead of "most tenderly" defeats the poet's strategy, which depends upon our believing that these swans are really humans trapped in bird bodies; the tenderest swan sounds inadvertently edible.)

It is at this point that Kate reveals some of her own orientation, for as narrator she begins to shift the moral ground of the poem. Lir's Children up to now have been presented as beautiful creatures in nature despite their imprisonment in swans' forms. When the sky is serene, Fionnuala's songs are hopeful. Their fate has been, not unnatural, but an awesome anomaly in nature. In their curse there was a blessing. With the fifth stanza Kate shows that the swan as bird is at home in its setting. She reinterjects also her own domestic preoccupation, and humanizes the "proud swan-father" and "mild swan-mother" as if using them as an object lesson for children, although her contrast would have been better served if she had emphasized the routine of fowl life. The birds' "household cares," their life "full of honest pleasure" make them sound not unlike the swan-children of

Lir, as described in the preceding stanza. However, in the following stanza, Kate as narrator tries to correct the possible confusion by showing us that the Children of Lir are out of place in nature:

> But alas! for my swans, with the human nature,
>   Sick with human longings, starved for human ties,
> With their hearts all human cramped to a bird's stature,
>   And the human weeping in the bird's soft eyes,
> Never shall my swans build nests in some green river,
>   Never fly to Southward in the autumn grey,
> Bear no tender children, love no mates for ever,
>   Robbed alike of bird's joys and of man's are they.

And for the next three stanzas three of the four human swans regret their life in the Never-Never land of the Celtic Golden Age. It is not so much that they want their enchantment lifted as that they (and by extension, Young Ireland visionaries of the turn-of-the-century) want to go back to a mythical past:

> "Sister," then saith Hugh, "most do I remember
>   One I called my brother, one, earth's goodliest man,
> Strong as forest oaks are where the wild vines clamber,
>   First at feast or hunting, in the battle's van.
> Angus, you were handsome, wise and true, and tender,
>   Loved by every comrade, feared by every foe:
> Low, low, lies your beauty, all forgot your splendour."
>   "Peace," saith Fionnuala, "that was long ago."

This stanza and the two that precede it fill their purpose perfectly. They reconstruct the aura of the exquisitely anachronistic Celtic Golden Age. The idiom and description belong to the Emain Macha ideal. The felicitous refrain is the narrator's transition back to present conditions. The Children of Lir are

left in their bittersweet eternal state. The privileged
narrator has sympathized with their plight, moralized
discreetly upon it. Now she withdraws and leaves us
with the fading twilight panorama. As twilight fades,
so fades the twilight kingdom. The landscape continues
to be beautiful, but night reasserts normal boundaries:

> Dews are in the clear air, and the roselight paling,
>   Over sands and sedges shines the evening star,
> And the moon's disc lonely high in heaven is sailing,
>   Silvered all the spear-heads of the rushes are—
> Housed warm are all things as the night grows colder,
>   Water-fowl and sky-fowl dreamless in the nest;
> But the swans go drifting, drooping wing and shoulder,
>   Cleaving the still water where the fishes rest.

Kate shows here her unfailing sense of reality. Even for
the mythology of young Ireland, she can suspend her
credulity only provisionally and for short periods of
time. Her fancy begins and ends in the matter of fact,
not only in this poem, but in her work generally. From
her inexhaustible fund of common sense she can see
enchantment as plainly diabolical, nostalgia as unpro-
ductive. Living creatures have their natural place and
can be happy only when fulfilling their natural roles.
Yeats, too, knew that normal life had its special
compensations, and he knew also that he was making the
otherworldly seem too attractive. It was, in fact, to
Kate that he wrote his often-quoted indictment of his
early poetry, March 1, 1888: ". . . it [his poetry] is almost
all a flight into fairyland from the real world, and a
summons to that flight. The Chorus to the 'Stolen Child'
sums it up—that it is not the poetry of insight and

knowledge, but of longing and complaint—the cry of the heart against necessity. I hope someday to alter that" (*Letters*, p. 47).

She lacked his self-criticism; he would have rewritten "The Children of Lir" if it had been his, preserving possibly only the first one-and-a-half and last four stanzas. She had neither the time nor the perfectionism to do it. It was not her aim to be the poet of the age but to say what she had to say and to make her father and friends happy.

"The Children of Lir," which pleased both popular and critical taste in the last decades of the nineteenth century, represents a poetic *persona* that is feminine: motherly, affectionate, and by virtue of these, condescending. As the 1890s began, Katharine Tynan had a fulltime freelance career underway. In 1891, for example, she published *Ballads and Lyrics* and a comissioned biography *A Nun (Mother Mary Xaveria Fallon)*. Her success had given her a great deal of freedom. But a Catholic rearing, a middle-class turn-of-the-century society could grant only a reprieve from marriage and motherhood, and her time was running out.

She would have to forgo being merely a daughter and a friend. That a person of such domestic interests would put off marriage until she was thirty-two is unusual. The most likely explanation is that the right person was not available at the right time. Not much is known about Henry Albert Hinkson. We know that she had to convert him to Catholicism. Hinkson was four years her junior, a barrister of the Inner Temple, a classics scholar with an M.A. from the Royal University of Ireland in 1890. In his lifetime, besides practicing

law and engaging in sports, he edited a book of verse,
wrote a treatise on copyright law, dashed off nineteen
novels and numerous short stories. He sounds like a
congenial mate for Kate, certainly an unexceptionable
suitor. Although his wife's reminiscences provide us a great
deal of information about her father, some allusions
to her children, extensive accounts of famous people who
came into her ken, she is extremely reticent about her
husband. (In this respect, she rivals Mrs. Wharton's
discretion about her ex-husband.) She never refers to
him by name; he is "my husband" or "one of us." Even
in the volume of memoirs in which his death occurs,
The Wandering Years, we deduce it solely because she
stops referring to him. The cause of death, the funeral,
her grief are all too private to bear relating.

Kate Tynan's nascent feminism, after all, while not
incompatible with domesticity, would keep her from
seeing marriage as the answer to a woman's life. By
May 1893, when she was married, she had succeeded in
a man's world. She knew that she did not have to rely
on a man for support, and her husband's difficulties
along these lines soon apprised her that it was imprac-
tical to do so. What her father did interested her partly
because it was he who was doing it. Otherwise, she may
always have found women more interesting than men
or may have cultivated such a strong interest in women
for the sake of her work that it amounted to the same
thing. Some women she positively adored. She never
saw another woman as a threat, a highly commendable—
and not too widespread—attitude. She mentions her
passionate admirations and friendships with a disarming
unconsciousness. For example, when writing in *Twenty-*

five Years of the daughter of a Oxford professor, she mentions in passing, "... every man in Oxford, ... was in love with her. A good many women, too, I should think" (p. 295). Another example is Lady Aberdeen, who was to be her lifelong idol. There was nothing about H. A. Hinkson that spurred her to such verbal rapture as that inspired by Lady Aberdeen, whom she met about the same time as she met her husband:

> My memory of her is that she was a big, soft young woman, with a boyish frankness and gaiety, added to the beautiful smile and voice so dear to her friends. She was deliciously friendly; such a warm, soft, large personality, like a rose ... She turned and took my hand in hers. Much water was to run under the bridges before the time came when her friendship was to irradiate my life, but I can remember how she wrapt me in warm kindness, ... how the charm of her personality delighted me. (*The Middle Years*, p. 77)

Hers was the feminism of a devout Catholic. We remember that a conventual life attracted her throughout her adolescence. At a Dominican convent such as that which she attended in Drogheda, there would have been attached to marriage a great deal of mystery not unmixed with dread. It was a sacrament to be entered into when a vocation was not possible. A nice girl was totally ignorant about what transpired between semi-sexless romantic infatuation and the sanctified blisses of motherhood. Kate was a very nice girl. Moreover, she could not have repressed altogether the example of an ailing mother who bore at least eleven children. There was nothing fearful and bewildering about the relationship between a father and a daughter, but the relationship between a father and

a mother she should not think about. A nice girl,
once conventually oriented, would not have desired
marriage as an outlet for her passion.

This was especially true since her father's home was so
nice, since he was so thoughtful, increasing his efforts
to make her home ever more comfortable. In one
of her last novels, *The Playground,* we see a devoted
father hurt and puzzled when his daughter finds an
acceptable suitor. The contextual details of this fictional
courtship (the farm near Dublin, the father's bluff
charm, the daughter's torn loyalties, her tasteful, cozy
sitting room, the persistence of the suitor) are presented
so convincingly that we suspect that the widow has
transposed her own situation after the deaths of both
father and husband left her free to reexamine it objectively. During her husband's lifetime, she permitted
herself these public recollections of leaving home
for her wedding: "My father, of course, was coming
with me to the boat. My sister woke up to say good-
bye—and it was over. I stepped up at the last moment
to look once again at my pretty room, the nest of love
which my father had made for me. . . ." She continues,
"I watched from the boat, as long as I could see it . . .
my father's figure in his whitish grey overcoat. He had
walked to the end of the pier to see the last of me.
I often wondered afterwards how I could have left
him". These lines hardly need comment.

But she had to leave home and she did. She had to
put her father in a secondary romantic place in her
heart and marry, for her domesticity and feminism
could be satisfied only by motherhood.

But for her, more than for most women, marriage

meant not so much the beginning of a new life as the poignant end of the old life. From the time she was fourteen until she was thirty-two, she and her father were each other's good listener. In "Everything that I Made" she avers that this habit of close communion persisted after his death: "And still I'm forgetting, ochone, that no longer you're near me,/And turn to you still with my tale, and there's no one to hear me." His example and precept had formed her. She could have said that the best that she was she owed to him. Her conversational charm, her loyalty to friends, her involvement with the disadvantaged, her kindness to animals, her affectionate, mothering nature—she had known the counterpart in him. His sympathy for man as underdog, his idealistic faith in the moral and physical values of country air, exercise, and nourishing food would persist into her last published editorials. He was proud of her gift, generous in supporting it. Moreover—and this made leaving home much more poignant—he was linked with Ireland, the idealized Ireland of her Parnellite fervor, of her first happy successes in literature. When she left him, she would leave them. Her poem to him called "To the Beloved" shows how aware she became of the pain and extent of her loss: "You were part of the green country," she specifies, "of the fields and mountains. . . ." And she concludes with the gnawing emptiness of desperate, irremediable homesickness:

> My heart seeks you in dreams and shadows,
> In dreams I find you, in dreams I kiss you,
> And wake, alas! to the lonely places.

2

1893–1919:
Wife and Mother

"We bore the Cross for each other, you and I."

As wife and mother, the dual role that elicited her best writing, Katharine Tynan saw herself as special perhaps, but never atypical. She titles a poem, which alludes to the shared sorrows of her marriage, "Any Wife," and concludes,

> Grief that binds us closer than smile or kiss,
> Into the pang God slips the exquisite bliss.
> You were my angel and I your angel, as he,
> The angel, comforted Christ in His agony.

There are only three facts about her wedding that Mrs. Tynan Hinkson considers interesting enough to relate: she was married in London; no member of her family accompanied her; since her hosts, Alice and Wilfred Meynell, did not have a clock, she was nearly late for the ceremony. Nothing is more important than marriage to her fictional heroines, but she is too discreet to tell us why she did not have an Irish home wedding. We know that her husband was attached to an army crammers' school in Kensington, that they started married life in a blossom-shaded cottage in Ealing, and that her father, who had to contribute to their support, made frequent visits, as did also the Meynells, the Yeats family, and John O'Leary.

She immediately resumed her work—writing, interviewing, free-lance reporting. Her pieces appeared regularly in *Sketch; Illustrated London News; The English Illustrated,* the weekly affiliate of the *Manchester Guardian; The Pall Mall Gazette; The Westminster Gazette; The National Observer;* and other periodicals. She worked on more serious pieces of poetry and prose at the same time.

She managed her career despite the anxiety of five pregnancies and the heartbreak of the deaths of her two first children. Through it all, she was helpmate and hostess and, when occasion required, a daughter again. Her husband was still doing work at Trinity College, Dublin, besides, we may presume, practising law and tutoring. Her circle of friends grew to include writers like Francis Thompson and Lionel Johnson and many helpful editors. Yeats continued to call.

As a journalist, she subscribed to the journalistic ethics of the day. When someone notable like Sir James Barrie said something quotable during what he believed was a personal visit but was an interview in disguise, she quoted first and apologized, if at all, only much later and only if she heard that the person was upset. Barrie was put off by her cavalier indiscretion, but apparently her visits to Christina Rossetti, by now a saintly invalid, caused no ill will. For her "Autolycus" column in the *Pall Mall Gazette,* she lifted her material from daily life and held her neighbors and servants up to her readers' amusement. She recounts with glee how she got by with such invasions of privacy.

Two of her first works to be published after her marriage give no evidence of newly found personal or professional maturity. She soon realized that she had no
flair for drama. *The Resurrection, A Miracle Play,*
which appeared in *Cuckoo Songs* (London, 1894),
tries to reconcile women to their role in life behind the
scenes. We know that playing behind the scenes was
never her role—probably one she never intended to
play. In any event, the concluding lines carry no conviction. The Angel admonishes,

> Woman was last beside the cross,
> And earliest in the garden was.
> Well she atones for Eve's great loss.

He tells the women in the cast and audience:

> Be virtuous wives and housekeepers;
> Keeping the home as sweet as Hers,
> The first of happy home-builders.

"Home-builders" was probably chosen for assonance
with "housekeepers" and "Hers," but if Mrs. Tynan
Hinkson meant it, she was being "chauvinistic" and
inaccurate. Mary and Joseph were not the first couple
to have or build a happy home, and Joseph the car-
penter was surely the builder, but Mrs. Tynan
Hinkson in giving Mary her due eliminates him from
consideration. Yet all in all, the whole was a sentiment
that would have gone down well with readers threatened
by suffragettes. This playlet errs only in pseudo-
simplicity. *Miracle Plays, Our Lord's Coming and
Childhood* (London, 1895) err in pretentiousness and
elegance. The sequence has six parts, each with prelude
and postlude poems. The stage directions, presumably

in an effort to preserve tone, are given with bogus
archaisms: "In the distance goeth the tall figure of
THE ANGEL. A woman standeth gazing after him." The
prelude to the Annunciation describes Dante Gabriel
Rossetti's *Ecce Ancilla Domini:* "Silver-pale his
[Gabriel's] lily," and the Holy Lands are inhabited
by models from the studio of Sir Hugh Holman Hunt;
Mary in the Visitation tells us that ". . . many a gold-
haired youth/Served me with milk and wine." Perhaps
works like these helped Mrs. Tynan Hinkson reconcile
herself to conjugal duties, as her convent instruction
would have termed them.

However it was, her volume *A Lover's Breast-Knot*
London (1896), dedicated to her husband and the son
whom they lost, their second to die in infancy, was
better than her preceding books in craft and sincerity. It
is clearly a touching example of self-therapy. She is make-
ing a desperate, determined appeal to her religion to sus-
tain her amidst these examples of cosmic injustice. "Love
Comfortless" is a simple ballad about her buried child.
She cannot bear to think of him as a cold lorn corpse,
so she must fantasize for herself a Nursery in Heaven.
The poem concludes,

> What wandering lamb cries sore distressed,
> Whilst I with fire and comfort go?
> O, let me warm him in my breast!
> *Ah, no,*
> *'Tis warm in God's lit nurseries!*

As for her own futile agony of pregnancy and frustrated
motherhood, her poem "Love's Rose" is a prayer:
"Blessed the will that doth accord/Me to grow roses
for my Lord."

The Hinksons moved away from the cottage that had seen their sadness, and settled near the Meynells in Notting Hill. However, their next two sons did not thrive in the city, and after many countryside and Irish vacations, the family grew used to happy stays in rented houses. They settled finally on Ealing, their base until 1911, when they returned to Ireland.

Despite frequent vacations in Ireland, despite what seems to be the instinctive gravitation of Irish to Irish in England, the Hinkson family lived in England for eighteen years. In many respects they identified with the English. They always thought of themselves as having a birthright to two homelands. This means that Mrs. Tynan Hinkson herself lived in England from the time she was thirty-two until the time she was fifty, the two decades when a person's opinions are definitively tried out and usually firmly established.

These mere facts of geography and age probably account for her failing to follow her fellow intellectuals of the Irish Renaissance in the paths their patriotism was taking them. After the grief that they all shared in the fall and death of Parnell, she was never to see things their way again. When she thought of herself as Irish, it was much as if she took pride in being from Kent or Wessex, and it did not preclude her feeling a nearly equal pride in being British.

This dual loyalty first shows in her attitude toward the Boer War, which depressed her, not as it did Irish patriots who saw the British as oppressors of freedom-loving, independent Afrikaans: No, she was depressed because at first the British suffered defeats. Queen Victoria's visit to Dublin in April 1900, which provoked Maud Gonne to insurrectionist activities, moved Mrs. Tynan Hinkson to sympathy, and she believed that the Dublin populace was touched by the visit as a gesture of reconciliation.

She and her husband thought of themselves as moderates, to use our term for the middle position that is open to practical compromise. They supported the enlightened colonialism of George Wyndham. However, from 1899 to 1914, the diorama of Irish politics shifted so rapidly that by contrast with those who supported the separation from Great Britain, the Hinksons appeared reactionary. During the years her husband was a Resident Magistrate in West Ireland, 1911–19, we have no evidence that they were embarrassed by having to support British policy.

For her readers, it was most prudent for her to be apolitical with a nuance of conservatism. She was taken up with her three lively, bright, good-looking children, and the necessity of keeping good servants so that she could earn the living, which, I suspect, her husband could probably only supplement. Some of the most ludicrous episodes in her reminiscences concern her servants, whom she wrote up in her columns and used in her fiction.

Her life was that of a middle-class matron, and her outlook was, also. For example, she balked at including passages from George Moore's fiction in an encyclopaedia that she was editing. Her remarks about servants in her reminiscences—even more, her delineation of servants in her novels—show her acute class consciousness. For example, Ralph Bretherton, hero of *A Midsummer Rose* (1913), is presented as a great humanitarian when he merely lets his manservant bring his wife and child on the premises.

Her account of the years between their remove to Ireland and her husband's death shows that she reacted to these critical times with annoyance and incomprehension. Annoyed when her family was not entertained by the Mayo gentry, she found the establishment of an officers' training camp nearby a welcome diversion. In *The Years of the Shadow* (London, 1919) she refers to the Easter Rising as a "rebellion."

For readers who wanted to believe in the stable Commonwealth, in a *status quo* only temporarily askew, she was comforting. In the first place, she does not question white superiority; for example, she praises Indian troops because they bravely follow white officers anywhere. No more does she question Christian superiority. Although, as we shall see later, her postwar novels are replete with anti-Semitic remarks, even when she is en route to the World Congress of Women in Rome, Spring 1914, in Lady Aberdeen's entourage, she cannot forbear wondering in print whether the German Jews who shared her restroom on the Paris-Rome Express ever washed. Nor does she question the essential rightness of class stratification, although she admires people who can rise above their original station. After the unnecessary deaths of the underprivileged in the Bachelor's Walk incident, July 26, 1914, her admiration in *The Years of the Shadow* is for those who restore order; Lady Aberdeen elicits all her attention: "I thought that she never looked more beautiful than that day in her deep mourning, the beautiful pearl ear-rings the one note of light in her sombre costume."

Nowhere does her acceptance of the values of her class emerge more strongly than in her extremely popular volumes of poetry, *The Holy War* (London, 1916) and *Herb O'Grace* (London, 1918). World War I, of course, became increasingly unpopular in Ireland and was bitterly opposed by the revolutionary elements. Yet many Irishmen fought in the war; Ireland suffered during the war. The ties with England were many. Mrs. Tynan Hinkson quieted the doubts of the Irish moderates. She reassured both English and Irish readers that the wartime sacrifices were holy. Her poems were favorites in both Catholic and Anglican pulpits.

Her diction is simple and natural. Mother of two sons in action, she can only be sincere. Our perspective on World War I and wars in general has changed so drastically that these books seem curiously dated and strange to us. The only poem that we can accept is "Haymaking, In Connaught, 1915," spoken by the farmer whose son is buried in France: "But the heart o' me's cryin' this minit,/For the boy that'll never come home". Her four poems on the Suvla debacle, August 15, 1915, where the Irish Tenth Division fought, console the bereaved with the claim that the victims have moved on to the gaming grounds of heaven. In "The Only Son" she suggests that God killed a boy in action so that his dead mother, who worried about him, would have company in heaven. In "To the Others" she stresses that her plight is that of all service mothers:

> Your son and my son, the downy things,
> Sheltered in mother's breast, by mothers wings,
> Should they be broken in the Lord's wars Peace!
> He who has given them are they not His?

She concludes, herself convinced, with exultation:

> Your son and my son, clean as new swords,
> Your man and my man and now the Lord's!
> Your son and my son for the Great Crusade,
> With the banner of Christ over them—our knights, new-made.

The second volume, written after Easter Week and two more years of World War I, would have to be more ingenious in finding cause for comfort. Mrs. Tynan Hinkson, whose sons had been wounded and had been missing in action, had to find satisfying rationalizations. "The Short Road to Heaven," for example, is the one taken by the fortunate heroes who died in battle:

> The young mothers' darlings, ah, who would bid them stay?
> The short road to Heaven's a green and pleasant way;
> They run singing and leaping, they will be in before
> The night darkens on them—and there's God at the door.

She even goes so far in "Comfort" as to remind her mothers that a son who dies in battle does not have to be shared with a wife:

> Now she need dread no more to grow
> Too old for him, she need not know
> The bitterness when he who was
> All hers turns to some younger face,
> And she his mother stands aside,
> Bidding her heart be satisfied.

She lets her readers entertain the pang of such a threat and continues,

> Now she's no longer dispossessed—
> For second best's but second best—

> He's here for all Eternity
> And she his one felicity.
> Her little son, as when he lay
> Small in her arms one heavenly day.

For such an unabashed document no Freudian comment is necessary.

Her own faith was justified. Her Pat and Toby returned and reentered British life. But her husband had died, and she and her daughter Pamela, her friend, confidante, and follower, began their wandering through England, Scotland, and the Continent. Ireland would be their homeland, but, except for intervals in rented houses, not their home.

Her best years and her best work were behind her, but she was too brave to admit it to herself. She had established her formulae during these years. She had discovered her incredible inventiveness in contriving plots for novels. She had begun writing historical romances and discovered her ingenuity in making history speak for itself. She had continued with her poetry and discovered in motherhood her best subject.

For example, *Love of Brothers* (1919), a novel set in Western Ireland, gives an authentic picture of upper-class ruthlessness and the gamut of skulduggery and decency found among the lower classes. The plot, intricate as it is, is actually a simple one by comparison with most of her novels, for she came to exploit more and more her ability to tell a tale and consequently had to slight characterization. Because of her goodwill and perhaps also because of her Catholic belief in repentance, she usually lets the villain redeem himself by the end of the novel, even if such a reprieve seems

totally inconsistent. Thus it is good strategy on Mrs.
Tynan Hinkson's part to have us too preoccupied by
the movements of the plot to notice that the characters
are acting out of character. In this novel, however,
there is a fair amount of verisimilitude if we accept
certain givens in Irish character. In the effective prelude
to the story, Patsy Kenny, a young farm boy, witnesses
a case of manslaughter: Lord Shawn O'Gara whips
Terrance Comerford's mount Spitfire and causes an
"accidental" death. When the novel proper begins,
Patsy is Lord Shawn's loyal studgroom and must
frustrate the periodic blackmailing of Baker, an
alcoholic gamekeeper, who was the other witness to
Comerford's death and whose wife and son Patsy adores.
Terrance's autocratic mother reappears with Stella,
his legal daughter by secret marriage to Bridyeen
Sweeney. (Mrs. Comerford had virtually confiscated
her granddaughter.) Stella promptly infatuates both
O'Gara's son Terry, whose parents are aghast at his
loving a girl presumably conceived out of wedlock,
and her real mother, who has returned to the community
as "Mrs. Wade." Stella repudiates her grandmother,
who tries to alienate her from her mother; the latter
then proves her own intrinsic worth—by producing an
authentic marriage license. Providence takes over
at this point: Baker breaks his neck; Lord Shawn,
trying to kill himself on a descendant of Spitfire, succeeds in making himself a permanent invalid. He even
confesses his misdeed to his wife, who forgives him.
Now Patsy can marry Mrs. Baker, and Terry can marry
Stella.

The givens here are the polarities of Irish character

and the moral code of a West Ireland community. It is readily noticed how closely Mrs. Tynan Hinkson adheres to her readers' expectations and prejudices. The upperclass is shown to have a mystique of nobility, permitting them extremes of behavior and attitude and requiring of us admiration and indulgence. For a superior person like Lord Shawn will have superior jealousy, superior fits of temper, and superior remorse. This "superiority" allows him, like Oedipus, to punish himself on God's behalf and circumvent the laws of man. The lower classes are shown to be a mixture of good, like Patsy and Mrs. Baker, and bad, like Baker. Although Stella and Bridyeen are presented as exquisite, sensitive, decent women, undeserving of social ostracism for any reason whatsoever, Mrs. Tynan Hinkson does not rest her case on their obvious merits, but on their unsuspected legitimate relationship.

The same givens hold in *Lord Edward*, subtitled *A Study in Romance*, which Mrs. Tynan Hinkson was writing in Mayo at the time of the Easter Rising. Lord Edward Fitzgerald (1763–98), aristocratic martyr of the '98 Rebellion, verifies in fact the polarities of Irish temperament that Mrs. Tynan Hinkson so often depicts in fiction. Lord Edward was an incorrigible romantic. As a professional soldier, he fought against the American revolutionaries and later returned to that continent for an exploratory expedition into Quebec in 1789. He was an appealing, albeit often frustrated, ladies' man, until true love tamed him. Upon his return to Ireland, this career officer who had tried to suppress the American Revolution sided with Wolfe Tone and the French in efforts to organize an Irish revolution.

Escaping the first attempt at arrest for treason, he was betrayed by the inevitable informer and died in prison from the wounds suffered in his capture. Gallant, brave, and unrealistic, Lord Edward was the same kind of hyperbolic personality as Lord Shawn in *Love of Brothers*.

Mrs. Tynan Hinkson adroitly links together the documents of the Fitzgeralds—letters, journals, and the like—and lets them expose themselves as kindly, patriotic, self-enthralled aristocrats, oblivious to the anomaly of their absentee patriotism. Unlike Maria Edgeworth, who would have turned such material into devastating multi-layered irony, Mrs. Tynan Hinkson, as kind to the dead as to the living, finds Lord Edward irresistible and leaves it to the reader to discern the egoism beneath his charm.

Her own personal charm, with its innocent normal egoism, comes through effectively in her domestic poems of this period. She can write nature poems with a pervasive mood. "August Weather," which can bear comparison to some of Robert Frost's New England poems, fixes the idyllic, unusually warm summer of her honeymoon in 1893 in these simple terms:

> Dead heat and windless air,
> And silence over all;
> Never a leaf astir,
> But the ripe apples fall;
> Plums are purple-red,
> Pears amber and brown;
> Thud! in the garden-bed!
> Ripe apples fall down.
>
> Air like a cider-press
> With the bruised apples' scent;

> Low whistles express
> some sleepy bird's content:
> Still world and windless sky,
> A mist of heat o'er all;
> Peace like a lullaby,
> And the ripe apples fall.

Here she achieves a happy suspension of cause and effect. There is no wind, no human activity, only the thud of an apple dropping from ripeness, with references to odor, temperature, and color. The discreet suggestion of the emotion proper to the setting is given in "Peace like a lullaby," presumably the secure feeling of a drowsy child being coaxed to sleep by a loving voice. It is a natural association for an Irish Catholic bride looking forward to motherhood. Frost, not only male and paternal but classically educated and profound, charges all of his superficially simple description with words permitting allegorical inferences, so in a poem like "After Apple-Picking" his ladder is pointing "Toward heaven still," he will experience "Essence of winter sleep." His comments upon this task make it possible to compare it with many other tasks, even to the entire "task" of living, for example, "I am done with apple-picking now" or "I am over-tired/Of the great harvest I myself desired." Mrs. Tynan Hinkson makes no pretensions to saying anything beyond the words themselves. A newly married woman soon to be fruitful, she sees the August harvest as something that nature arranges by its own tranquilizing processes. She is unquestioning, contented to be a part of the scene that she describes.

To write even one such good nature poem is a feat.

It is not a feat, however, that distinguished her work from that of other poets, for English and Anglo-Irish poetry is rich in nature poems.

Her distinctive poems are those on the eros of motherhood. A well-bred woman of her class cannot speak too openly of love, even conjugal love. If Mrs. Tynan Hinkson had for her husband feelings comparable to Elizabeth Barrett's for Robert Browning, she was too inhibited to write them down. But she did not feel inhibited about speaking openly on the ecstasy of motherhood. On this subject she can let herself go without offending her readers. These poems are honestly, innocently sensual. "The Meeting" is a casual encounter with her six-year-old:

> As I went up and he came down, my little six-year boy,
> Upon the stairs we met and kissed, I and my tender Joy.
> O fond and true, as lovers do, we kissed and clasped and
>   parted;
> As I went up and he went down, refreshed and happy-
>   hearted.

She praises God for having allowed her to know motherhood and to write about it in "The Senses":

> I thank Him for my hands so feat.
> "Now write!" He said; and they have writ,
> That know the feel of roses sweet
> And the child's cheek so exquisite.

Her four-year-old son is the object of her prayer in "The Desire":

> Dear God, You give me from Your skies,
> A little heaven, all mine, to hold,
> As Mary once her Paradise,
> Just four years old.

She blissfully exults in being the goddess of her children's world in "The Mother":

> Great passions I awake that must
> Bow any woman to the dust
> With fear lest she should fail to rise
> As high as those enamoured eyes.

She intends to profit from the responsibilities of this transient idolatry, for she continues,

> Now for these flying days and sweet
> I sit in Beauty's Mercy-Seat.
> My smiles, my favours I award
> Since I am beautiful, adored.

The anxiety, of course, is one of her burdens, as she brings out in "The Sick Child," also a prayer:

> Give me back my boy, I pray,
> Turbulent, of yesterday:
> Not this angel, like a sword
> In his mother's heart, dear Lord!

Nor does she pretend that children are not often in the way. As a professional writer, she knew, in advance of the latter-day career woman, the mixture of guilt and annoyance caused by children's demands. "The Mother's Hour" presents the conflicts of co-existing adult and childhood worlds:

> My little son would fain
> Go from his mother never;
> Leaves me with tender pain,
> As parting were for ever.

> I who have business,
> The little cares of living,
> Though small hands cling and press,
> I send him from me grieving.

Not that she actually fears that an accumulation of resentment will lead her son to reject her, but she is aware that some day she will be less important in his life. She concludes:

> Time, there may come a time
> He will not so approve me.
> This is my golden clime,
> In which the children love me.

We can be thankful that Mrs. Tynan Hinkson was unaware of Freudian psychology when she was composing these aptly titled *Innocencies*. If she had been more knowledgeable, she might have been more reticent and denied us her best verse.

These poems have very simple meters and use language that she could have used in conversation. They bear the stamp of sincerity, and there is every reason to believe that they reflect her most intimate and deeply felt erotic experiences.

There may be no more sensual poetess of motherhood. The purely feminine cast of her writer's personality may have been a deficiency when she was writing a third-person novel; it was an experiental drawback certainly when she is commenting upon the Easter Rising or poeticizing the glories of wartime combat. But for poems on motherhood she could only be authentic.

She is true to her training. Motherhood and marriage are responsibilities sanctified by God's Plan. Her poems are assertions turning into prayers. Perhaps more candid than she realized, she sees herself as the more essential member of the couple, for she states in "Any Woman," "I am the pillars of the house," "I am the fire upon the hearth," "I am the house from floor to roof," and concludes, "Take me not till the children grow!" But her experience with marriage must not have disappointed her expectations of it. On the contrary, it must have verified her convent ideal of it. In "Any Wife," quoted at the beginning of this chapter, she recognizes in marriage a bond of mutual need and support: "We bore the cross for each other, you and I,/ When through the darkest hour, the night of dread,/ I suffered and you supported my head." She recognizes that a man of her class, with its Anglo-Saxon code, has his particular difficulties in enduring pain: "Because a man can only bear as he may,/And find no tears for easing, the woman's way." For a devout Catholic like her, God is literally her witness: "Thou knowest, Lord,/What we endured for each other: our wounds were red/When he suffered and I supported his head."

Her husband's death in 1919, coinciding with the end of World War I, a state of insurrection in Ireland, and the maturity of her children, marked the end of her best role, the one that society considers a woman's preeminent role. A widow at fifty-eight, she must enter the era of Emancipation as an elder stateswoman and write her heart out for herself alone.

3

1919–1931:
The Career Woman

"I shall die young though many years are—"

One of the many attractive features of Mrs. Tynan Hinkson's character is a canny, feminine toughmindedness that concentrates on the immediate task and leaves no time for self-pity. The type of direct, unreflective practicality often ascribed to women, she eminently embodied. Some widows go under, some discover resources that they did not know they had. Mrs. Tynan Hinkson faced widowhood with a sense of loss—we would have slight grounds for suspecting that the Hinksons were not companions and helpmates—but with no sense of helplessness. During marriage, she had more than paid her own way. The demands on her now would be less heavy, if anything, for her sons, veteran officers soon to be embarked on their own careers, were fully independent; her daughter Pamela, manifesting her mother's talents already, promised to be as plucky and resourceful. Mrs. Tynan Hinkson had to a remarkable degree the faculty of considering a disadvantage an opportunity. Her eyesight, defective since early childhood, as noted, became more problematical. She often had to rely quite literally on other people for guidance. Even this definite handicap she could interpret as a special dispensation. In the prayer "The Purblind Praises the Lord," alluded to earlier, she asserts that she is blessed to have a tree appear as a "burning bush of green," to be aware of birds as "an enchanted choir," to see cherry blossoms as "an avalanche/Of snow-white flower on flower." Her clouded vision is in fact a gift:

> I miss the common and the dull,
> The small details of things,
> And only keep the beautiful,
> The stars, the flowers, the wings.

If she has the determination and faith to conceptualize partial blindness so positively, it is not surprising that she can face widowhood and the Troubles, from her point of view a civil war, by making herself a screen of memory, the good days that came before, and give thanks for it. She had lived "In a green world withouten any war" and so she can say, "I was fed full with bliss past my desert,/And when grief came, was comfort to my hurt."

Her activity during the last decade of her life is staggering. Some of her adventures she recalls in *The Wandering Years* (Boston, 1922), roughly 1918 to 1922, and *Life in the Occupied Area* (London, 1923), roughly July 1922 to May 1923, some of them are reflected in feature stories. A genial guest, she was lionized in Britain and Scotland. She traveled widely in continental Europe and made three extensive visits to Cologne. Although she and Pamela tried to stay impartial during the Troubles and could hope by virtue of their neutrality to keep a safe base in Ireland, this proved to be too difficult. Thus, although both of them wrote regularly for Irish newspapers during this decade, their base was most often in England, and it was there that they were living when Mrs. Tynan Hinkson died, on April 2, 1931, after a short illness.

Her capacity for hard work continued with no discernible slackening. In *The Years of the Shadow* (Boston, 1919) she had commented, "I am not especially proud of this facility of mine; it has produced a good deal of honest work, with, of course, a good deal of necessary pot-boiling, and it has made some few people happy beside [*sic*] myself." Writing was her way of life by now, a pleasure and an occupation as well as a source of income. In *Life in the Occupied Area* she records, "Between July, 1922, and May, 1923, inclusive I wrote without effort and sheer joy in the doing, three novels, a play, a book of 'Memories' of dead friends, and the book that is under your eyes."

As a journalist she is most persuasive when writing directly from her own domestic experiences, least persuasive when writing on subjects that need documentation, observation, and background. In *The Years of the Shadow,* she candidly admits that she wrote eleven articles on the Women's Congress in Rome (1914) without attending its sessions. At the time her eyesight made it impossible, she says, to see beyond her nose. In the context of history, this 1914 Congress was merely a well-intentioned pastime for upper middle-class women. We can readily sympathize with Mrs. Tynan Hinkson's desire to bluff her way through her reports and to spend her time and eyesight more profitably. And her conviction that American church women are aggressive and selfish would still find sympathizers. At the same time we are somewhat amazed that she expects us to take any of her "eyewitness" accounts seriously.

However, in *Life in the Occupied Areas,* more significant aspects of modern history are involved, so her reliance on hearsay—on English speakers in a German-speaking community, occupied by the French army before she and Pamela left Cologne—is a more incriminating datum in her reporting technique. She is understandably touched by German children and the Germans' love of children: "When one kneels at the same altar with a people and loves their children, one cannot hate that people." For the mother of two World War I Allied officers, she seems uncommonly trusting: "All uniformed men in Germany have a protecting, a caressing air with them. . . ." Some of her generalizations are close to prejudice. For example, of religion, she says, ". . . I think I may advance it that a Catholic population is usually more friendly and expansive than a Protestant one, not because of the Catholicism but because of the racial characteristics which go with the religion." Her prejudice against Jews seems to be based on her conception of ethnic habits, rather than on religion. She accepts her landlady's opinion that postwar inflation is being caused by Jews (p. 270). Of her Jewish friend Mr. Apfil, she hastens to assure us that he was "quite another type of Jew from the hook-nosed, dingy fraternity." She understands the Cologne population's shock and resentment at the French Occupation's using African troops, but she excuses the Ally on the grounds that these troops "are, of course, not a negroid type, but very handsome with fine features." We in turn can excuse her on the grounds that this type of reporting was outside her competence and that, dependent upon others for information, she had been misinformed.

Where she knows what she is talking about, her basic kindness toward humankind and animals is quite apparent. On the lot of animals she is most eloquent. As a farmer's daughter, albeit one whose rearing protected her from a great deal of farm activity, she is aware that animals must serve human life, but she wants them raised kindly and slaughtered humanely. In an editorial in *The Irish Statesman* (November 15, 1924), she comments on cattledroving conditions with a threat: "All those years the cries of the dumb-animals have been going up to Heaven for vengeance." In this same editorial, she adheres closely to her upper middle-class views of class structure when she places the blame for the abuse of animals on her own class: "Cattle-drovers were, in my knowledge of them, a very low order of beings. The responsibility of their evil deeds must, I think, rest largely with the decent people who tolerated and employed them."

The lot of Irish school children moves her deeply, as we should expect. In an exposé editorial in *The Irish Statesman* (October 29, 1927), she has documented her plea with an account of their long hours, the distances they must trudge, the inadequate food in their lunches, the inadequate heat and ventilation in their classrooms. She admonishes, "There is no real

virtue in accepting for one's self or one's children conditions not fit for human existence. God did not will
consumption and rheumatoid arthritis. Ignorance and
carelessness willed them." She adds, "May it [electric
light] flash light, warmth and cleanliness into our
homes, our schools, our public buildings—and, dare
I say it?—our Churches."

Her last remark, which criticizes conditions in
Irish churches, is telling, for it leads us to our discovery
that where the welfare of a child or woman is concerned,
she moves far beyond the accepted moral confines of
her class. We are not surprised when she writes in
The Irish Statesman (June 30, 1928) about the need
for humane working conditions for shop girls; she
makes their plight her subject in the novels *Lover of
Women* (1928) and *Grayson's Girl* (1930). We might
suppose that any unselfish woman might have said
as much. But her views on infanticide and unwed mothers
would be congenial to Women Liberationists of the
1970s. She asks for mercy for the unwed mother and
recreates for the reader the pity due weakness and
loneliness. In three 1929 articles in *The Irish Statesman*
(May 4, December 7, December 14), she is openly
indignant at the Irish laws, which favored the man and
permitted him to escape the consequences of his acts.
"I venture to say that in most cases of infanticide a man
should be in the dock with the woman." She has
learned a lot about the world since she advised women
readers in *Cuckoo Songs* (1894), to "Be virtuous
wives and housekeepers;/Keeping the home as sweet
as Hers."

And she has become alert to other injustices about

her. In *The Irish Statesman* (August 10, 1929), she speaks out against capital punishment on the occasion of the announced hanging of a man and a woman. Despite her belief in innate class differences, she is benevolently inconsistent. Commenting on a poor village that has its unemployment temporarily alleviated by the Shannon River development, she asks, "Why do they not hate us, going by, well-fed, well-clad? We exist on the forebearance, the generosity of the poor!" [*The Irish Statesman*, June 15, 1929].

Although journalism was the most public of her activities as a committed professional writer, she used many of her novels of this period as a forum also. *Denys the Dreamer* (New York, 1920), *The Golden Rose* (London, 1924), *Lover of Women* (London, 1928), *The Rich Man* (London, 1929), *The River* (London, 1929), *Grayson's Girl* (London, 1930), and *The Playground* (London, 1930) show her ideas constructively in action. Perhaps their closeness to her most deeply felt concerns partly accounts for their continued interest. As I shall show in more detail in the next chapter, Mrs. Tynan Hinkson has a penchant for sensational plots couched in nonshocking language. An Irish setting, and a plot tied in with one of her projects for human betterment ensure her authenticity.

Denys of *Denys the Dreamer* is an engineer who turns his gifts to reclaiming the West Ireland estates of his benefactor. His tasks are complicated as much by the ignorance of the natives, who think his draining of the bogs has brought on a drought of Saint Senan's Well, as by the harshness of the elements in this section of Ireland. Denys is Mrs. Tynan Hinkson's example of the vision, patience, and stamina needed when one sets out to improve the human lot.

The Golden Rose demonstrates the pettiness of class prejudices in West Ireland as they are exacerbated by the heartaches of World War I and the reversal of Irish attitudes toward the war. The title character is Carmel O'Reilly, daughter of the parish dispensor, who fights with his four sons for the British. Dr. O'Reilly is invalided out after Easter Week and loses his job to a Sinn Feiner. While he is under virtual ostracism by the Irish for his British loyalty, his daughter suffers from the snobbery of the Anglo-Irish gentry, who will not countenance her relationship to the local peer, now an amnesia victim. Mrs. Tynan Hinkson must resort to Providence in the form of an automobile accident and the peer's self-effacing fiancée in order to effect a happy ending, but not before she has made a good case for the destructiveness both of class bigotry and of narrow patriotism.

The Lover of Women and its sequel *Grayson's Girl* present the case for enlightened management in department stores that employ women. Simon Grayson, the hero, when six years old witnessed his drunken father's fatal fall from a ladder. Since his father in his maniacal torture of his wife had just killed her dog and canary and was intending to kill their son, the death was providential. Simon, educated by his mother's steadfast admirer, went into merchandising partly from flair and partly because of his mother's admonition to be kind to women. The book is marred by Mrs. Tynan Hinkson's conviction that German Jews are to blame for unfair labor practices, for as soon as Simon takes away the power of his chief's Jewish managers and puts his own fraternal, humane practices into effect, not only are the clerks better cared for but the store profits increase. In the sequel, Simon dies from battle injuries in World War I, but his own prosperous profit-sharing London department store is run by his wife for their daughter, who has a bent for practical philanthropy. The readers meanwhile have seen the way a store should be run, the way women clerks should be treated.

The intervening *The Rich Man,* which shares some of the characters of the two preceding novels, is a plea for practical philanthropy, shown to be extremely viable when it supports cooperative enterprises. When a somewhat under-witted Irish socialist assassinates the self-made British millionaire, the victim sees the justice of his violent death and conceals the identity of his attacker. Having thus taken his death as his due personal punishment, the millionaire entrusts to his son, the philanthropist of the title, the reparation of his business sins.

If in these three novels Mrs. Tynan Hin.. is careful not to give away her lack of knowl.ge about profit-sharing stores and cooperative enterprises, in *The River* she moves her platform to human relations, about which she is better informed. The river of the title is the chasm separating the Galway Black Protestant gentry and Catholic gentry. The river is bridged by the efforts of Kitty Adair, who comes to stay with her cousin Alice, the spinster dowager of the area. From the standpoint of conventional characterization, the novel falls apart when fantasy-ridden, self-pitying, complacent Alice is turned into a heroine and given a happy ending, for a reader's automatic reaction is to reconsider and decide that the novelist must have considered Alice's failings virtues all along. Actually, what we have is an example of Mrs. Tynan Hinkson's personal compassion. She cannot hold Alice responsible for unthinking class and religious bigotry inculcated by tradition. She will not deprive even a character in fiction of a chance for happiness when she considers this imaginary person good at heart.

The Playground, drawing extensively on her life before marriage and arguing the case for equal opportunities for all children, is perhaps her most touching, socially committed novel. The setting is Dublin and London, 1887–1919 (the period extending from her first publications to her husband's death). Through the character of John Tracey, a Dublin slum urchin whose father is a drunken paperhanger, she shows how proper environment, education, and encouragement can not only prevent an otherwise wasted life but can benefit humanity at large also. John is taken in by the Barton family, where the father is modeled after Andrew C. Tynan and where the housekeeper-hostess daughter is even called Katie. John is trained in horticulture and biochemistry in England. Successful there, guided by one of the philanthropists from *Lover of Women*, he uses his success, reputation, and prosperity to organize playgrounds for Dublin slum children in memory of his deformed sister, Nonie, and his brother, Christopher, a casualty in World War I.

In showing the terror and abuse caused by drunken men, the disease-breeding conditions of Dublin slums, the toll wreaked upon the poor slum mothers, who are the ineffectual martyrs of the environment, Mrs. Tynan Hinkson is fearlessly graphic. She does not analyze the causes of degradation. Her stated antipathy to labor leader James Larkin, whom she considered a demagogue, might lead us to deduce that she could not have believed that unrestrained capitalism or British colonial mercantilism was in any way responsible for the demoralizing conditions of the Dublin disadvantaged. But as to the effects of the system, whatever it is, on children and women, she is alert, responsive, and aggressive.

These remarks hold generally for all her committed writing, whether reported as fact or dramatized as fiction. She does not concern herself with the probable roots; her only cure is a hope that people who are advantaged will be unselfish. She considers it her role to move in quickly with maternal solicitude, using her pen to bestir the consciences and open the pocketbooks of her more fortunate readers.

She saw life, in short, as possessing the potentiality for happiness; earth, as possessing the potentiality for paradise. Whereas her feature writing and fiction showed what needed to be changed, her poems showed what should be kept. In this respect, she had nothing new to say. All her deep experiences were behind her. Her best inspiration—her children when small, cuddly, and dependent—could not be recaptured. Since she willed to be faithful and unquestioning, she could not admit to the anguish of old age and approaching death. She could only repeat herself. Her example is more inspiring to us than her actual work of this period.

Ernest Boyd had claimed in *Ireland's Literary Renaissance* that by *New Poems* (1911) "there is hardly a line that could not have been written by the average young lady and gentleman with a facility for rhyme." Herbert Gorman, reviewing *Twilight Songs* (1927) for *The New York Times* (August 21, 1927) begins by saying, "She has done better work than this," and ends by saying "The pulse [poetic] beats feebly, however." But it was not her aim to be original or profound, but to support herself and share her sentiments.

Her ideal life is one that she holds up confidently for every reader's approval. The best time of life, what every woman looks back on or forward to, is the family in the first years of marriage: home, husband, children, friends. Her prayer "She Asks for New Earth" is quite explicit:

> Give me a little house for my desire,
> The man and the children to sit by my fire,
> And friends crowding in to us, to our lit hearth—
> For Thy new Heaven, Lord, give me new earth!" (p. 70)

4

The Writer as
Exemplary Woman

Little sisters, the birds:
We must praise God, you and I—
You, with songs that fill the sky,
I, with halting words.

In this gentle sermon that Yeats commended, "St.
Francis to the Birds," Kate Tynan internalized her
favorite saint as a winsome *persona*. She admonishes
herself and her readers as the saint admonished the
birds. Speaking as St. Francis, she avers, "All things
tell His praise." She refers to the young of the birds
tenderly as "children":

> When the soft heads overbrim
> The brown nests, then thank ye Him
> In the clouds of heaven.

The birds as mates are husband and wife to her, and
their roles are clearly defined: "Husbands, be ye kind
and true; Be home-keeping, wives—." The Voltairian
solution sounds appealing in her terms:

> Stay at home and keep the nest;
> Fly not here and there in quest
> Of the newest thing.

She could not heed her own advice, and she did not regret her life. Still, as "She Asks for a New Earth" indicated, she never found cause to alter her ideal. Today, nearly ninety years later, no one could claim that the advice of this poem published in 1884 should be totally discounted.

Although the proportion of women readers whom she would represent has probably decreased, the number may well be greater. Since only one of her books, the collection of poems edited by Monk Gibbons in 1963, is readily available, her readers among the generations since her death is largely limited to students of the Irish Renaissance. She is, perhaps unfairly, both dated and placed.

It may be a coincidence, but one of the results, if not one of the planned effects, of seeing herself as a representative woman is that she never expressed a really distinctive self. In that respect, her work is remarkably even. Her corpus contains no quintessential piece, no major work. It is consensus that poetry is her best genre. Pamela Hinkson says that her mother had a particular fondness for her historial romances. She bombarded the market with novels. All are of a piece. We could be missing vast amounts of her fiction and still have an accurate estimation of what she had to say and how she would say it. If, as her daughter remembers, she had the most space of any single author in the British Museum, it is safe to assert that she was the most prolific member of the Irish Renaissance. Much of her writing, as she herself admitted, had to be potboiling. As it happens, she wrote very few entirely satisfactory works. So, if we can talk about commendable characteristics of her work as a whole, we can find few

thoroughly commendable works. She was too closely tied
to her class to transcend it.

We are dealing with a woman who wrote quickly,
often hastily, in order to get into print (and get paid)
as soon as possible. Since she had to please her public,
it was fortunate that most of the time her code and theirs
were in agreement.

Although she could be quite explicit when describing
substandard living conditions, she is careful not to
shock the conventional reader. She avoids the sexual
and the vulgar. Occasionally she will remind us that she
is sparing us details. In *Lover of Women* (1928), she
assures us that in Simon's marriage to a woman four
or five years older (as was the case with Mr. and Mrs.
Hinkson), the bride "had nothing to complain of the
ardour of his kisses." In *The Admirable Simmons*
(1930) we witness this intimacy between husband and
wife: " 'Poor Edward!' she said slipping an arm about
his neck and leaning towards him till his head was
against her soft breast" (not only a motherly gesture,
but the description makes it sound as if the wife is somewhat larger than her husband, like a mother and her
adolescent son). When the title character of *Miss Phipps*
(1925) insults Delia, the heroine, we are told that Delia
knows such words are awful but does not know what they
mean. Mrs. Tynan Hinkson knew that this kind of
reticence was unfashionable, but she knew also that she
was writing for women like herself. In *The Wandering
Years,* she recalls that Arnold Bennett, mindful of her
reputation, protected her from risqué conversation.
What she wrote in *The Irish Statesman* (September 29,
1928) about the Irish Censorship Bill, which other

prominent Irish writers found objectionable, was in fact the popular opinion then and still remains so. "Personally," she says, "I should be well content to see much of the English Sunday newspapers banned, not so much because of the immorality as because of the horrors." She does not spare her colleagues: "Personally I should not object to the exclusion of many modern novels, both Irish and English." She herself always wrote from an extremely severe inner censorship.

This does not mean, however, that she did not take up threatening behavior or work out fantasies that must have been veritable nightmares. She spun plots that could exceed any grisly feature story in sheer extent of horror and brutality. Her plots typically follow a pattern of delayed achievements: protagonist X, after overcoming innumerable formidable obstacles, succeeds in performing task Y and in winning reward Z. Any of these algebraically indicated elements may be multiple. There may be more than one hero or heroine working together or on parallel tracks. All will receive rewards, and, typically, if at all possible, their antagonists will have a change of heart that will allow them to share in the reward. There are few unmixed villains, and Mrs. Tynan Hinkson is ever alert to extenuating circumstances to provoke our pity and understanding. The pattern that I have just described could be applied to many novelists: Hawthorne's novels fit the pattern perfectly; so do most works by Thackeray, Meredith, and George Eliot, to restrict the example to works that Mrs. Tynan Hinkson would know. Where her plots differ from theirs is in the accumulation of obstacles to be overcome and the *faits divers* incredibility of them. (Undoubtedly, she worked for a specified length and was obliged to add gratuitous complications.)

Some of the typical givens in her fiction show how well she manipulated—unconsciously, I am convinced —the threats and fears of a middle-class woman's imaginary life. The chief of these is the threatening female. Although we have seen in "The Comfort" in *Herb O'Grace* that Mrs. Tynan Hinkson is capable of telling a mother that having her son die in battle spares her the misery of having to share him with a wife, generally she takes the side of the younger woman against the man's mother or mother surrogate. The man's mother can be so very pathologically possessive that when it happens that she is not, it is presented as a surprising exception to the rule. The beastly mother-in-law is a common bugaboo, and Mrs. Tynan Hinkson can be sure of first arousing and then allaying a fear if she introduces a vicious mother and lets the wife-to-be win. She has a more curious, perhaps even unique, female villain who stands in for the shameless Jocasta: a vampire nurse. This terrifying victimizer stalks through novels set after World War I and keeps her veteran victim bound to her through exploitation of his illness, which, by the time the younger woman comes along to rescue him, is largely a psychological dependency. The older woman relies on medicine, magic, and more experience, and will accept morbid dependency when erotically colored filial love is no longer forthcoming. The younger woman represents normal activities and confidence-inspiring innocence. (Like Melville's Captain Delano in *Benito Cereno*, her "bluff" succeeds because she is not aware of the dangers around her.)

The second threat in a woman's life is the disappointing male. After all, society sets up the expectation that marriage will be a full and happy state, and a woman has her marriage only fifty percent within her control. At best, the disappointing male, as Mrs. Tynan Hinkson portrays him, is the husband not sufficiently resourceful to earn a steady income. In novels set after World War I, such a man is not condemned, because he has been debilitated or bestialized by his battle experiences. Or he can be a well-meaning drunkard or blackguard. (Men, she implies, are such weak creatures.) Mrs. Tynan Hinkson democratically finds drunkards and blackguards in all social classes. It is not an oversimplification to say that her expectations for men are lower than her expectations for women. When a man is weak, a woman must compensate for his weaknesses with a smile and a prayer; when a woman is weak, another woman must be called in to help the man concerned. A man is threatening in the long run simply because he is biologically stronger; a woman can usually outwit him, and only a woman can rout the female villain.

What the heroine, and the likable secondary women characters as well, must fear is the threat she offers herself. Her own looks are her greatest source of anxiety. She may not be pretty, and in this case she really cannot expect a man with his innately superficial value system to marry her and give her the certification needed for full social acceptance and motherhood. Whether or not she is older than her husband, she may look older than he or, what comes to the same thing, lose her looks (aging is judged solely by figure and face) and, inevitably, her husband's affections as well. Mrs.

Tynan Hinkson promises her good-natured, plain, motherly girl readers, by means of such an example as Juliette Durrell in *Castle Perilous* (1928), that beautiful first wives die and leave behind a chastened husband, whose vision is now cleared to spiritual beauty. Mrs. Hinkson repeatedly reassures her women readers who are the mother of several children, by such an example as Sheila Hunter in *The Admirable Simmons* (1930), that they are so unmitigatedly gorgeous that their only concern should be not outshining their teenage daughters.

A woman's anxiety about her looks had been exploited by novelists a long time before Mrs. Tynan Hinkson; both Balzac and Jane Austen handle it adroitly. A new source of anxiety was the wave of female emancipation immediately preceding and following World War I. The new freedom had new risks as its corollary, and Mrs. Tynan Hinkson, whose own daughter was (and is) emancipated, intrepid, and attractive, was understandably worried about the implications. Since she wants no change in her conventual moral code and since ignorance of the ways of the world is an essential part of the code, she is faced with a dilemma that only Providence can resolve. (An unmarried woman must be innocent, and she cannot maintain a properly naïve expression if she knows very much.) Her attractive, candid, and naïve young women must have an attractive young Irishman materialize at continental intersections to rescue them from difficulties that information and prudence could have prevented.

After all, Mrs. Hinkson on the basis of her own experience believed that existing systems needed only their optimum operation for the New Earth. In her

view, apparently, there really were enough philanthropists to go around, and, with a little sensible care
(she favors cosmetics) and good luck, any woman
could keep her looks until her husband died.

I have spoken now and again in this essay of class
attitudes. I have not yet dealt with class tastes. Mrs.
Tynan Hinkson was an exemplar of good taste. She
comments lovingly on clothes, home furnishings, down
to the proper color for bath salts (to judge from *Grayson's
Girl,* they should match the bathroom curtains). She
almost preaches on daily bathing, sound nutrition
(her pet characters are never too harassed to relish a good
breakfast), and proper ventilation.

Her taste in decorating styles, exclusive of feminine
dress, in which she is very modish, is conservative. This
is not surprising, but it does call for comment. With her
dim eyesight, she could not be expected to find the plastic
arts exhilarating. She occasionally uses a family portrait
as a prop, but art has no emotive effect as a motif.
In *Grayson's Girl* (1930) her favorite philanthropist
character, who could have been a patron of Post-
Impressionists, decorates with reproductions of Sir
Hugh Holman Hunt's "The Light of the World" and
John Millais's "The Order of Release." (She was bound
to appreciate a picture showing a plucky redhaired
woman with babe in arms bailing out her husband
from the straits into which his rashness had got him.)
Her taste, in short, remained that of her girlhood.

It did so even though she had opportunities for
travel and was lionized by the well-to-do. It did so
even though her friends in the first wave of the Irish
Renaissance were in the vanguard of the plastic arts

as well as the verbal arts. Through the Yeats family she would have heard of the painting and decorative developments of Bedford Park, which went far beyond the developments of Pre-Raphaelitism and Art Nouveau. Lucien Pissaro lived in Bedford Park. Her friends Lily and Lolly Yeats were part of William Morris's atelier. John B. Yeats painted portraits of both her and her father. Jack Yeats, the best Irish painter to date, while never directly connected with continental schools, by the late 1920s had developed an Expressionistic style. She was in the London environs when the Tate Gallery opened in 1897. She was a friend of Hugh Lane, who coaxed her Yeats portrait away from her, and she must have followed the controversy when his French Impressionist collection was exhibited in Dublin in 1908. She did not leave England until after the important Post-Impressionist show in the winter of 1910–11. She and Pamela made extended trips to Germany, center of Expressionism; France, center of Cubism and Surrealism; and Italy, center of Futurism and Metaphysical painting. As well informed as she was, she had to be aware of these movements, if only because her sophisticated daughter described them to her. But the vanguard arts were either too taxing for her eyesight or too incomprehensible for her taste. As a journalist and as a fiction writer, she kept silent about the new art, plastic and verbal.

Deprived by her handicap of intense pleasure in the plastic arts, she seems not to have compensated by an increased cultivation of the other arts. Edith Wharton's young ladies, Henry James's as well, have at least finishing-school accomplishments. They draw, play the piano, and sing. Mrs. Tynan Hinkson's knew how to dress and manage a house and garden. Her taste in music seems to have remained with the ballads and popular songs of her youth. The only music to which she repeatedly refers is that of the birds.

Dance and drama seem outside her interests also, even though she was her father's theater companion, even though she was young and of an age to be enthusiastic in the days of the Golden Age of the Abbey Theatre. She and her husband were living near London during the heroic age of Synge, so she could not have been intimately involved. But there is no record that the urban arts of Dublin and London ever figured in her life after she married and left home. She certainly does not promote the dramatic forms in feature story or fiction. The feminine sensitivity to art, the feminine receptivity to the new in art, that we expect in American and continental women of her class, is almost totally lacking in her.

No, for her the exemplary woman is truly a culture-bearer. She is one who preserves what was best from the past. She does not renew culture or infuse it with innovations. She makes it more comfortable, more environmentally healthy, more morally rigorous. Her center of radiation is the foyer—of fact or spirit.

It would appear as a corollary, in her case, that for matters outside the foyer Mrs. Hinkson habitually relied on outside sources of information. The home was her province even in her career, shrewd as she was in managing the latter. For matters outside her direct experience she must have been repeating secondhand opinions. In the interest of plausible dialogue in the

mouths of her male protagonists, she retails views
that are racist, anti-Semitic, anti-Evangelical. She is
sufficiently prejudiced that she repeats such views in
her own voice in her memoirs.

She as a woman was always concerned about her own
family and all members of humanity whom she could
imagine as part of her family. There is no need to
belabor her inability to realize that non-Christians
and nonwhites form part of the family of mankind.
She was a superior example of her class, and we cannot
expect her to repudiate its mores. She believed in them.
She was loved by her readers because she was one of
them.

Her view of her faults would not be the same as our
view of them, but she was always a devout Catholic
and she asked God's mercy for them. Her capacity for
honest humility never failed her. Her plea through
her *persona* St. Francis to us, her readers, imposes
compassion upon us:

> And remember me,
>   Poor Brother Francis, who
>   Loves you, and gives thanks to you
> For this courtesy.
>
> Sometimes when ye sing,
>   Name my name, that He may take
>   Pity for the dear song's sake
> On my shortcoming.

5

The Exemplary Woman as Writer

> *God gave a gift of singing to my mouth,*
> *A little song and quiet that was heard*
> *Through the full choir of many a golden bird.*

Kate Tynan's poetic *persona* is indeed her most endearing, whether the mask is her kind Irish face or a congenial one borrowed from history. The self that wrote her poetry distilled what was the best in her. The class prejudices that mar her fiction, the self-promotion and self-justification that make her memoirs unwittingly ironic, these rarely intrude in her poetry. As the epigraph above suggests, she saw herself as a thrush whose song was heard despite the competition of a richer-voiced artificer like Yeats, a Byzantium craftsman. Her preposition *through* suggests that the ear had to be especially attuned to register her sound because it was of a different, thinner quality. When we characterize her poetry, we find ourselves using "appealing," or "touching." We could say "delicate," if we are careful to specify that we mean "light" and "tinkling." We could say "charming" in the sense of having a charm of its own. We could say "smooth" in the sense of "easy rhyme" and "dependable rhythm."

Literary history may decide now that her reputation

would be better if she had never published fiction and had restricted herself to a single volume of memoirs. But her family needs did not permit that—nor did the demand of her vast and loyal public, who still remember her fondly. She did what she set out to do. She was a success by the most realistic measure.

As a result, she forces us to consider the case of the woman writer. She wrote about a representative woman's experiences, her own; thus far, her procedure is commendable, for it gives her work authenticity. Nevertheless, although her range of experiences through career and travel made her—or could have made her—far from typical, she accepted for herself and her work the traditional limitations of female experience and insight. She exploited them profitably; we have seen more than enough examples of that. Thus she would try to coerce us to judge her work by separate—and less demanding— criteria for literary excellence.

I have applied these shorter yardsticks to her work. But I have not forgotten, while pointing out the extenuating circumstances, the larger standards of excellence. I should not, because there are too many cases of women writers who have qualified as major writers without special dispensations. Maria Edgeworth's *Castle Rackrent* exposes the mythical Anglo-Irish good old days as relentlessly as Mark Twain's *Huckleberry Finn* exposes the myth of the antebellum South. Any writer of first rank conforms his or her own context to a personal vision. It could be claimed that her contemporaries Mrs. Wharton and Miss Lagerlöff used their fiction for a backward glance. The former, however, objectively judges the society of her debutante days;

the latter used the fantasizing faculty of her compatriots as an aid in holding our credulity. Miss Viebig, Miss Hugh, and Countess Pardo Bazan saw their own times with a jaundiced eye with an aim to social betterment, but an aim that they do not let get in the way of psychological credibility. Among Mrs. Tynan Hinkson's fellow countrywomen, Somerville and Ross, members of the Anglo-Irish upper class, concealed their class attitudes behind a witty *persona*. Lady Gregory, who had an excellent ear for native speech, literally effaced herself in retelling legends or spinning a playlet. These could be said to have a view of the "mere" Irish comparable to Faulkner's or Eudora Welty's view of the Southern Black, that is, that of a compassionate, wry outsider. Mrs. Tynan Hinkson had a formidable facility. She probably had, or could have, cultivated the skills of any of these writers, but she accepted for herself the narrower vision, the fainter voice, the nonchalant style that she thought excusable in a woman writer.

She set out to be a minor writer. AE linked her name favorably with Christina Rossetti's. Miss Rossetti's religious orientation was attractive to Kate Tynan. I have compared her in passing with Elizabeth Barrett Browning, who could write from marital experience. Yet, both as Katharine Tynan and Mrs. Tynan Hinkson, she set too close a goal for herself for her ever to equal their achievements. She never developed the former's virtuosity in form and inventiveness and in poetic substance; she diverted her own inventiveness into fiction when with patience she quite probably could have written excellent long narrative poems. She never allowed herself to express the latter's intensity or passion;

I could never prove that her romance was not so tender
and satisfying, but she was too inhibited, too well-bred
by her own definition, to verbalize it. Her elder friend,
Alice Meynell, who set out to be a good poet, at least
has a niche as a minor poet. She is a better religious
poet than Mrs. Tynan Hinkson. As a convert, she had at
one time to assess Catholicism, and her poetry reveals
more impressive intellectual scope and emotional depth.
Mrs. Tynan Hinkson preferred to rest on the surface. She
could not in fact see far, and she restricts her spiritual
vision analogously.

In the end, she excels only other Irish poetesses, not
poets, of her own generation. Susan Mitchell, Dora
Sigerson, and Eleanor Hull do not equal her in skill or
substance. This is a very modest field of excellence.

But these remarks, while denying her a place as an
exemplary writer, do not keep her from being an
exemplary woman. She spoke for the daughter who
never forgot her father, the wife who respected her
husband, the mother who was foolish about her
children, the widow who knew how to manage. She was
the Anglo-Irishwoman loyal to both countries when
they were at war with each other. She was Anglo-Irish
and Catholic at a time when the rising Catholics tended
to feel increasingly alienated from the Ascendancy, whose
members were traditionally Church of Ireland. Her
unquestioning faith, nurtured by a convent education
and lifelong practice, did not set her apart from her
own Anglo-Irish middle class since she shared its other
concerns, and it inspired confidence in the aspiring
Irish middle class. She had stayed with a woman's lot,
so men did not need to fear her, yet she had exploited

it in the ways permitted by men. She was bound to be popular, and she was industrious enough to satisfy the appetite that her work whetted. She was good to her listeners, her children, her animals. She thought of herself as a mother. She tended her readers and she tended her hearth: "Some came and drank of me from near and far—/I was born under a kind star."

Selected Bibliography

KATHARINE TYNAN'S WORKS:
A SELECTED LIST

Louise de la Vallière and Other Poems. London: Kegan Paul, 1885.
Shamrocks. London: Kegan Paul, 1887.
Ballads and Lyrics. London: Kegan Paul, 1891.
A Nun (Mother Mary Xaviera Fallon). London: Kegan Paul, 1891.
Irish Love-Songs. London: T. F. Unwin, 1892.
Cuckoo Songs. London: Elkin Mathews, 1894.
Miracle Plays. London: John Lane, The Bodley Head, 1895.
The Way of a Maid. New York: Dodd, Mead and Company, 1895.
An Isle in the Water. London: A. and C. Black, 1896.
A Lover's Breast-Knot. London: Elkin Mathews, 1896.
The Wind in the Trees. London: Grant Richards, 1898.
The Queen's Page. New York: Benziger Brothers, 1900.
Poems. London: Lawrence and Bullen, 1901.
The Sweet Enemy. Philadelphia: J. B. Lippincott, 1901.
The Golden Lily. New York: Benziger Brothers, 1902.
The Great Captain. New York: Benziger Brothers, 1902.
A Daughter of Kings. New York: Benziger Brothers, 1905.
Dick Pentreath. London: Smith, Elder, 1905.
For the White Rose. New York: Benziger Brothers, 1905.
Innocencies. London: A. H. Bullen, 1905.
Julia. Chicago: A. C. McClurg, 1905.
Her Ladyship. London: Smith, Elder, 1907.
A Little Book of Twenty-four Carols. Portland, Maine: T. B. Mosher, 1907.

The Story of Baron. Chicago: A. C. McClurg, 1907.

Twenty-one Poems. Dundrum: Dun Emer Press, 1907.

The Lost Angel. Philadelphia: J. B. Lippincott, 1908.

The Book of Flowers, with Frances Maitland. London: Smith, Elder, 1909.

Ireland. London: A. and C. Black, 1909, 1911.

A Little Book for John O'Mahony's Friends. Portland, Maine: T. B. Mosher, 1909.

Mary Gray. London: Cassell, 1909.

Peggy the Daughter. London: Cassell, 1909.

Betty Carew. London: Smith, Elder, 1910.

Freda. New York: Cassell, 1910.

New Poems. London: Sidwick and Jackson, 1911.

Paradise Farm. New York: Duffield, 1911.

Princess Katharine. New York: Duffield, 1911.

The Story of Cecilia. New York: Benziger Brothers, 1911.

A Mésalliance. New York: Duffield, 1913.

A Midsummer Rose. London: Smith, Elder, 1913.

Miss Pratt of Paradise Farm. London: Smith, Elder, 1913.

Rose of the Garden. Indianapolis: Bobbs-Merrill, 1913.

Twenty-five Years. London: Smith, Elder, 1913.

The Wild Harp. London: Sidgwick, Jackson, 1913.

Irish Poems. New York: Benziger Brothers, 1914.

The Curse of Castle Eagle. New York: Duffield, 1915.

The Flower of Peace. New York, Charles Scribner's Sons, 1915.

Flower of Youth. London: Sidgwick and Jackson, 1915.

The Holy War. London: Sidgwick and Jackson, 1916.

Lord Edward. London: Smith, Elder, 1916.

The Middle Years. London: Constable and Company, 1916.

Late Songs. London: Sidgwick and Jackson, 1917.

Herb O'Grace. London: Sidgwick and Jackson, 1918.

Miss Gascoigne. London: J. Murray, 1918.

Love of Brothers. London: Constable and Company, 1919.

The Man from Australia. London: W. Collins, 1919.

The Years of the Shadow. Boston: Houghton-Mifflin Company, 1919.

The House. London: W. Collins, 1920.

Denys the Dreamer. New York: Bengizer Brothers, 1921.

The Second Wife. London: J. Murray, 1921.

The Wandering Years. Boston: Houghton-Mifflin Company, 1922.

Evensong. Oxford: Blackwell, 1922.

Pat, the Adventurer. London: Ward, Lock and Company, 1923.

They Loved Greatly. London: E. Nash and Grayson, 1923.

The Golden Rose. London: E. Nash and Grayson, 1924.

The House of Doom. London: E. Nash and Grayson, 1924.

Memories. London: E. Nash and Grayson, 1924.

Life in the Occupied Area. London: Hutchinson, 1925.

Miss Phipps. London: Ward, Lock and Company, 1925.

The Moated Grange. London: W. Collins, 1925.

The Face in the Picture. London: Ward, Lock and Company, 1927.

The Respectable Lady. London: Cassell, 1927.

Twilight Songs. New York: D. Appleton, 1927.

Castle Perilous. London: Ward, Lock and Company, 1928.

The House in the Forest. London: Ward, Lock and Company, 1928.

Lover of Women. London: W. Collins, 1928.

A Fine Gentleman. London: Ward, Lock and Company, 1929.

The Most Charming Family. London: Ward, Lock and Company, 1929.

The Rich Man. London: W. Collins, 1929.

The River. London: W. Collins, 1929.

The Admirable Simmons. London: Ward, Lock and Company, 1930.

Collected Poems. London: Macmillan and Company, 1930.

Grayson's Girl. London: W. Collins, 1930.

The Playground. London: Ward, Lock and Company, 1930.

Poems. Edited by Monk Gibbon. Dublin: Allen Figgis, 1963.

Her Father's Daughter. New York: Benziger Brothers, n.d.

SECONDARY SOURCES

Compared to other figures of the Irish Renaissance, Katharine Tynan can be said to have received no critical study of her work.

Boyd, Ernest. *Ireland's Literary Renaissance.* rev. ed. New York: Alfred Knopf, 1922. (Barnes and Noble reprint, 1968.)

Gibbon, Monk, ed. "Introduction," *The Poems of Katherine* [sic] *Tynan.* Dublin: Allen Figgis, 1963.

Gorman, Herbert. "Countee Cullen a Poet First." *The New York Times,* August 21, 1927 (section III), p. 17.

Hone, Joseph. *W. B. Yeats, 1865–1939.* London: Macmillan Company, Ltd., 1943.

Maguire, C. E. "Incense and Breath of Spice." *The Bookman* (June 1931), pp. 375–80.

Russel, George [AE]. "Foreword," *Collected Poems* [of Katharine Tynan]. London: Macmillan and Company, Ltd., 1930.

Yeats, W. B. *Autobiography.* New York: The Macmillan Company, 1936. (Garden City, N. J.: Doubleday Anchor Book, 1958.)

———. *Letters to Katharine Tynan.* Edited by Roger McHugh. New York: McMullen Books, Inc., 1953.